THE Tramways OF Wolverhampton

Eric T Challoner

In this publication, the author traces the history of the Wolverhampton tramway system from its earliest horse-drawn beginnings in 1878, through the subsequent electrification of the routes in the early 1900s, with the controversial decision to use a system that proved to be unique to the town (and indeed the world), resulting in the town having to endure route isolation from other tramway operators until the eventual, and somewhat inevitable, wholesale conversion to the more conventional form of overhead wire operation in 1921. The gradual contraction of the system and change to trolleybuses between 1923 and 1928 is also covered in detail.

The continual political battle fought over the years with the British Electric Traction Company Limited tramway empire, whose various companies effectively surrounded Wolverhampton, has not been ignored, and there are fascinating insights into the daily life of the systems, in particular the Wolverhampton District Electric Tramways Company and Kinver Light Railway.

When you are old and grey and full of sleep, and nodding by the fire, take down this book and slowly read, and dream of the soft look your eyes had once, and of their shadows deep.

William Butler Yeats
1865-1939

The author, who was born in 1947, has been a keen transport historian and researcher for many years. Though currently living in Wellington, Shropshire, Eric spent his formative years in Wolverhampton, later becoming a member of the Transport Group at the Black Country Living Museum, where several of the tramcars that once plied our streets can now be seen in regular operation.

Published jointly by:

The Light Rail Transit Association
138 Radnor Avenue
Welling
DA16 2BY
www.lrta.org

and

Trolleybooks
156 High Street
Bildeston Suffolk IP7 7EF
www.trolleybooks.co.uk

Designed by Sherbert Design
www.sherbertdesign.co.uk

Printed by Latimer Trend & Company Limited
Estover Road
Plymouth
Devon PL6 7PY

ISBN 978-0-948106-50-7

Other titles by this author include:
Trolleybus Memories Wolverhampton. Published by Ian Allan in 2007. ISBN 0-7110-3214-9
Farewell the Derry Road. Published by Colourpoint in 2010. ISBN 978-1-906578-76-3
Trolleybus Days in Wolverhampton. Published 2017 by the Light Rail Transit Association. ISBN 978-0-948106-51-4

COVER PICTURES

Front upper: *A view of Cleveland Road depot in late 1902. As the fleet grows, the available space is rapidly being taken up; cars 17 and 19 arrived in August of that year.*
Front lower: *An inward bound tram is seen near St Jude's church. From the postmark showing through, the illustration appears to be from a popular postcard of the time.*

Rear Upper. *Wolverhampton 49 waits at the museum's village terminus, with a departure for the museum entrance.*
Rear Lower. *At the Black Country Living Museum WDET tram 34 approaches the crossing with the trolleybus route, on a service to the village.*
Author's collection

Contents

Whilst every effort has been made to ensure accuracy, the passing of time, coupled with fading memories and conflicting dates in a number of other sources, has resulted in areas of uncertainty, with some details open to question. The author would be pleased to accept any new information.

Though endeavours have been made to trace the copyright holders of photographs used in this book, many of the pictures in private collections bore no clues as to the photographer's identity and it is hoped that any owners recognising their photographs will accept this statement in lieu of a full acknowledgement.

I am indebted to John Hughes, Deryk Vernon, Cliff Emery and David Smith for all their help, and would like to place on record my thanks to them for their assistance and continuous encouragement in dealing with my queries, during the preparation of this book. I hope that the end result will give the reader some indication of the multitude of emergent companies that appeared on the scene towards the end of the 19th Century and show how they variously came together to provide a cohesive whole, resulting in a picture of tramway operation in and around the environment of Wolverhampton

In memory of my father, Cyril Thomas Challoner;
Proud to be a Wolverhampton man, he delighted in
telling me tales about the town he loved and grew up in.

Preface

Wolverhampton was one of the most important towns in the history of tramway operation in the British Isles, being a leader in innovation and design. The decision by Wolverhampton Council to use the unique Lorain system of current collection can, in retrospect, be seen as both a bold move in its day and perhaps one that bordered on recklessness in view of the complete lack of operating experience in any other town. If the short-lived line trialled in Washington DC in 1898 is discounted, it remains the only application of this system anywhere in the world.

Under the control of Mr W A Luntley, its first General Manager, the Wolverhampton system was steadily extended to encompass the main areas of housing development, in some cases terminating on what was the edge of open countryside. Tragically, Mr Luntley was to lose his life in 1915 and the early development work that he oversaw was continued by his successor, Charles Owen Silvers MIEE, MInstT, appointed with effect from 1 December 1915; Mr Silvers would later find fame for his own pioneering work with 'rail-less' cars and became regarded as the driving force behind the move to transform their image into that of the trolleybus that we know today.

Wolverhampton's trams enjoyed a variety of operational surroundings, with the run westwards down the tree-lined Tettenhall Road, with its genteel housing, and the equally pleasant Lea Road, which curved its way quietly past semi-detached Victorian houses, contrasting sharply with the 18th century terraces and back-to-back housing to be found on the routes to Wednesfield and Willenhall. Again, the journey to Hunter Street in Whitmore Reans passed close to the West Park and often afforded an interesting cameo to travellers, of middle- and upper-class Victorian social life. The line to Bushbury completed the picture of variety, passing the thriving and industrious Great Western Railway Locomotive Works on the Stafford Road, complete with all the noise and pollution associated with such industries.

The author, who was born in New Street, Wednesfield, within yards of the original tram terminus, has had an interest in electric traction for many years and started researching the town's tramways back in the early 1960s, drawing on recorded notes and extensive research, assisted by a surprising number of surviving artefacts; the Lorain contact studs and tramway rails in particular remained embedded in the floor of Cleveland Road depot until the end of the trolleybus system in 1967.

The history of tramway operation is traced from its early beginnings with the horse drawn service to Newbridge in 1876, through the development of the early 1900s with the ill-starred Lorain System and on into the battles fought with the BET empire, in their attempts to obtain running rights over the Corporation's lines, culminating in the Council's decision to convert to overhead electrification in 1921, only a few years before closure and conversion of the routes to operation by trolleybus. BET group tramway operators adjacent to Wolverhampton are also given good coverage.

Colour illustration of Car 10. Cliff Brown collection courtesy John Hughes

A section of original tram rail from the Wolverhampton Tramways Company. Author's collection

The changeover to trolleybus is covered in detail within the book, ably supported by a wealth of tramway operational information, including fleet lists, extensive route maps of Wolverhampton and the surrounding systems and BET boundary junctions, with an extensive selection of historical photographs that fully complement and support the written history of Wolverhampton's tramway system.

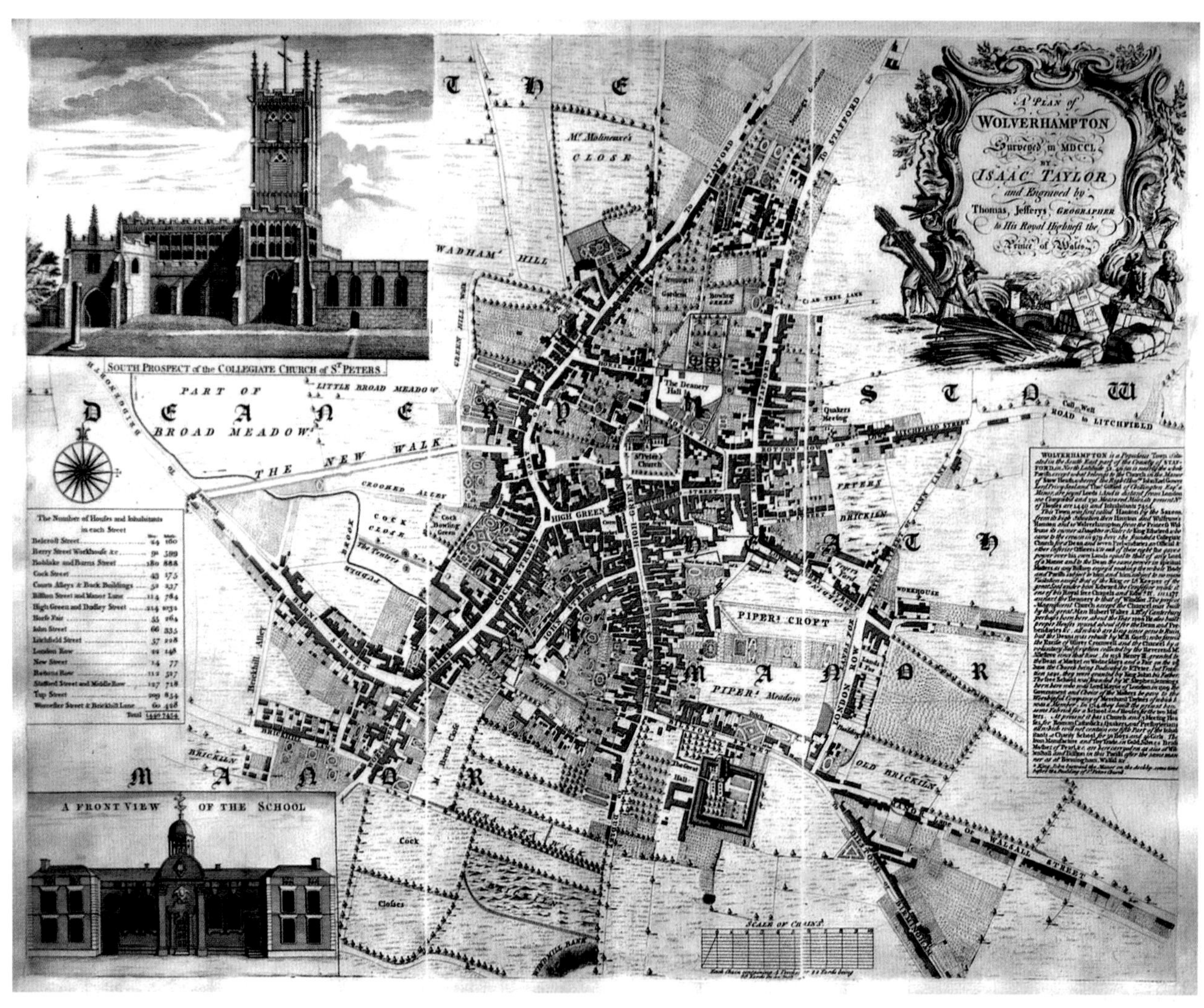

A plan of Wolverhampton, as surveyed by Isaac Taylor in 1750. High Green would eventually become Queen Square and Darlington Street would not make an appearance until 1823, the ground be granted to the Corporation by Lord Darlington.

Above: High Green Wolverhampton in the 1700s

Right: Victoria Street

Author's collection

CHAPTER 1 Introduction: Tramway Origins and the Early Pioneers

Wolverhampton lies 120 miles north of London, on the edge of the Black Country between Stafford and Birmingham, with the border county of Shropshire on its western flank, and sits some 650 feet above sea level on a bed of red sandstone. The town was granted city status on 18 December 2000 and currently has a population estimated at 240,000. For the purpose of this history, all text refers to the 'town' as indeed it was in the days of tramway operation; likewise, all reference to money is shown, where appropriate, in the pre-decimal style of pounds, shilling and pence, to reflect the coinage in use at that time.

The town was first established as a settlement in 985 A.D. At this time, King Aethelred II (The Unready) who reigned 979-1013 and 1014-1016, occupied the English throne. The younger son of Edgar, he became King at the age of seven, following the murder of his half-brother Edward II in 978 at Corfe Castle by Edward's own supporters. He was known as Edward II to distinguish him from Edward the Elder c. 874/877 - 924 and in later writings he was often referred to as Edward the Martyr, reflecting the circumstances of his demise. In 985, King Aethelred granted lands in the area to his sister Lady Wulfrun. These lay in the small settlement known as Heantun. In 994 Lady Wulfrun endowed a monastery and church there.

The settlement subsequently became known as Hampton and the prefix Wulfrun was added in time to avoid confusion with similarly named places nearby, the name eventually becoming Wolverhampton; it is generally accepted that this evolved from the Anglo-Saxon Wulfruneheantun, meaning Wulfrun's high or principal enclosure or farm. A new church was built around 1190 and re-dedicated to St Peter in 1258, during which time a charter was granted by Henry II to hold a market in the town, that has continued on a weekly basis ever since, the ensuing wool trade continuing to prosper until the middle of the 16th century, when it declined with the growth of woollen cloth production in Yorkshire. The town became involved in the development of numerous different trades, and by the middle of the 19th century, Wolverhampton had become a centre for the manufacture of tinplate, ironmongery, locks and japanware.

By 1730 the town had a population of over 7,000. There is documentary evidence for what was probably a very basic stagecoach service three times a week between Wolverhampton and Birmingham. The first daily horse drawn coach service began in July 1783, and linked the town to neighbouring Walsall. Further services followed and by 1818 connected Wolverhampton with destinations as far away as Manchester, Bristol and London. By the early 1830s, long-distance services were declining in the face of expanding railway competition, leaving only the local services, themselves under increasing threat from private horse buses. Records show that George Bayley started the first recorded omnibus service in 1833, using a nine-seat coach. In 1835 he was followed by John Doughty, who operated a service to Birmingham, being joined on this route in 1836 by the Midlands Omnibus Company and the Birmingham Omnibus Conveyance Company. After the introduction of horse trams, horse drawn omnibus services soon faded from the scene, being unable to compete financially.

Railways were to reach Wolverhampton on 4 July 1837, with the Grand Junction Railway opening a station at Wednesfield Heath, a mile out of the town. It did not make a great impact on the area, and the passenger service closed on 1 January 1873, although the goods and parcels service managed to remain open until 4 October 1965, when the remaining section of the station was demolished. The Shrewsbury & Birmingham Railway opened its Wolverhampton Railway Works in 1849, becoming the Northern Division workshop of the Great Western Railway in 1854, under the control of the Locomotive Superintendent, Joseph Armstrong. This was closely followed by the opening of their Low Level station, in 1855, the London & North Western Railway High Level station having pipped them to the post, by opening for business in 1852.

Tramway origins and the early pioneers

And so to the advent of the tram! There is some obscurity surrounding the origin of the word, with learned persons variously suggesting that it comes from either the Swedish word "tromm" meaning a log, or more possibly the German word "traam" meaning a beam; in the middle ages lines of wooden beams were often laid in mines to ease the transportation of tubs containing ore. The earliest record pertaining to a tram comes from 1555, when one Ambrose Middleton bequeathed 20 shillings for the improvement or correction of the tramway from the West End of Bridgegate in Barnard Castle, County Durham. By the 17th century, tramways paved with wooden beams were in general use for horse-drawn wagons carrying coal from the mines, with trucks fitted with metal wheels being used in the German Tyrol.

By 1734, cast iron wheels with an inner railway type flange were to be found around Bath, Somerset, with cast iron rails replacing wooden beams in 1767 at the Coalbrookdale Ironworks in Shropshire. In 1776, Benjamin Outram became one of the first people to use iron rails extensively when he constructed a tramway for

An early picture of the Oystermouth Railway and Tramway Company. Author's collection

the Duke of Norfolk's colliery at Sheffield, effectively creating the first recognisable railed tramway system.

It is believed that the idea of laying rails into the public road was first thought of by an Irish engineer named Edgeware in 1802. The first true passenger-carrying line was the Oystermouth Railway and Tramroad Company, in the parish of Oystermouth at Mumbles Bay, near Swansea, Glamorgan, which was incorporated in 1804. In 1806 horse-drawn goods traffic began, the main cargo being limestone. The area then began to develop in its own right as a tourist resort, changing the industrial character of the district, and in 1807 the line became unique by offering the first regular rail passenger service in the world. The line survived until 1960; its closure dented the local economy and has been deeply regretted ever since.

Development in the UK rapidly followed across the country. On 30 August 1860, a tramline was opened at Birkenhead, Cheshire, being quickly followed in 1861 by two lines in London, one in the Bayswater Road on 23 March, with the other in Victoria Street on 15 April. None of these lines lasted for any great length of time, the London lines in particular suffering from serious opposition due to the damage caused to private coaches, as the lines were of a raised step type. Later horse tramways used the more familiar grooved rail, flush with the road surface.

The Tramways Act of 1870 appeared on the statute books on 9 August that year. It was designed to provide a measure of protection for those local authorities whose areas would be served by growing number of intending tramway operators and encourage their participation, also giving the authority an absolute veto on proposals they did not like, together with the power to make compulsory purchase of any tramway system after 21 years of operation. Additionally, the Act required operators to repair and pave the roadway between the rails and to a distance of 18 inches either side of the track; on double-track sections the entire road effectively became the operator's responsibility.

CHAPTER 2 Horse Drawn and Steam Tramways in Wolverhampton

By the middle of the nineteenth century, there was evident need of a more co-ordinated public transport system to link the outlying areas with the centre of Wolverhampton.

A letter from a Mr Webb in London dated 22 September 1876 was received by the Town Clerk, intimating that a group of influential gentlemen was interested in constructing a tramway in Wolverhampton. A meeting subsequently took place with an engineer, Mr Joseph Kincaid, on behalf of the London group and was followed by a further letter of 13 October detailing three proposed routes: to Newbridge, Willenhall and Bilston. This resulted in the incorporation on 14 December 1876 of the privately-owned Wolverhampton Tramways Company, with registered offices at 3 King Street, London. The Wolverhampton Tramways Order 1877 was confirmed on 23 July 1877, clearing the way for construction to start.

The Wolverhampton Tramway Company's intentions would of course also come under the remit of the Tramways Act of 1870. Although this was a private venture, Wolverhampton Council had declared an interest from the start and retained the option of compulsory power of purchase of the business within ten years of opening, or after the twenty-first year of operation. Also, there was a ruling that any lines laid in High Street could not be used for passenger carrying without first getting the consent of the Council. By December 1877, the Company's head office had moved to 23 Queen Victoria Street, London.

The contractor, W T Mousley, who hailed from Clifton, commenced work on the first line, to Newbridge, early in 1878. Lines set to a standard gauge of 4ft 8½in were laid between Queen Square, in the centre of town, and Newbridge to the west; Queen Square had received its name in 1866 to commemorate a visit by Queen Victoria,

A view of Queen Square in 1899, with horse trams and buses well patronised, in a busy scene. Cliff Brown collection cty John Hughes

when she unveiled a statue of her late husband, Prince Albert, mounted on a horse. Prior to this the area had been known as High Green.

The proposed line of the route had been facilitated in no small measure by the creation of Darlington Street in 1823; following a request to Lord Darlington, a parcel of land belonging to him was sold to the Town Commissioners for £350 per acre and used to form a new road running directly from Queen Square to Chapel Ash, thus improving access to the Tettenhall and Holyhead Roads and providing a more direct route. John Moreton surveyed the land and construction was placed in the capable hands of the Borough Engineer, John Worrallow, a man who also enjoyed the dubious distinction of simultaneously holding down the posts of Chief Constable, Sanitary Inspector, Weights and Measures Inspector and Markets Manager! Prior to construction of this road, the best way into the centre of town from the west had been by a very circuitous route along Salop Street and Victoria Street.

Progress was rapid and following an inspection and trial run on 30 April, the service was opened with the first horse-drawn service leaving Queen Square at 8.00 a.m. on 1 May 1878 for the journey to Newbridge, a fare of 2d being charged. With the opening of the Tettenhall line, depots were provided at the foot of Darlington Street, at number 45 and at the Newbridge end of the line, next to 144 Tettenhall Road. On relatively level ground, a single horse could pull a tram carrying around twenty people. However, an additional chain horse would be needed and fetched from the depot to assist in the steep ascent up Darlington Street to Queen Square.

A tramcar is seen approaching Queen Square as it reaches the top of the climb up Darlington Street, while another tram descends towards Chapel Ash. North Street is on the right.
Author's collection

The venture proved to be a success, and further lines were laid down towards Willenhall, completed by mid-May and opened on 6 June 1878, and to Bilston,

The location is by St Jude's Church, on the Tettenhall Road in the late 1890s. The 4ft 8½in-gauge (quite evident in this view) tramway terminated at Newbridge. The road has changed not much over the last 120 years and there is much that is still recognisable.
Cliff Brown collection cty John Hughes

A late 1870s view of Queen Square, showing the 4ft 8½in tram track curving into Dudley Street. This was part of the system used by the horse-drawn services of the Wolverhampton Tramways Company from 1 May 1878 until 12 June 1902. Author's collection

opened during July, with an extension to Moxley, plus an additional depot there, in August 1879. The three routes, largely single track with passing loops, had cost around £70,000 to construct and the length of the system was a little less than 10 miles, of which just over four were inside the Borough boundary.

At the town end, the three routes departed from separate starting points; the Tettenhall line running from Queen Square along Tettenhall road to the boundary at Newbridge, while the Willenhall cars terminated in Queen Street but loaded and ran from Horseley Fields to a point adjacent to Willenhall Market in New Road, although some evening services loaded in Queen Street before setting out towards Willenhall. The Bilston service started alongside the Queen Street Chapel, the loading point being a little nearer to High Street in the evening, and ran along Bilston Road to the centre of that town, terminating at the junction of Lichfield Street and Church Street, outside the Town Hall. The extension to Moxley connected end-on with the Wolverhampton service, running down Oxford Street to the junction of the Wednesbury and Darlaston roads. Tram lines had also been laid in High Street and, as previously mentioned, were used purely for stock movements from Darlington Street depot and saw no regular service working other than the occasional special.

The Tettenhall terminus at Newbridge with car 21. The two horses are being transferred to the front for the return journey. The side road is Newbridge Crescent.

Cliff Brown collection cty John Hughes

On 20 December 1879, a second Company, the Dudley, Sedgley and Wolverhampton Tramways company, was formally registered, and using the powers granted by the Dudley, Sedgley and Wolverhampton Tramways Order of 1880, a single-track horse tramway line was constructed between Dudley and Wolverhampton.
On 7 May 1883, using seven double-deck open-top cars provided by Ashbury, the horse-drawn services to Dudley

Newbridge terminus with car 24 and its motive power! The conductor is H Icke and the driver J Brueton.
Cliff Brown collection cty John Hughes

Horse tram 23 inward bound in Chapel Ash, circa 1900. This tram is preserved at the Black Country Living Museum.
Author's collection

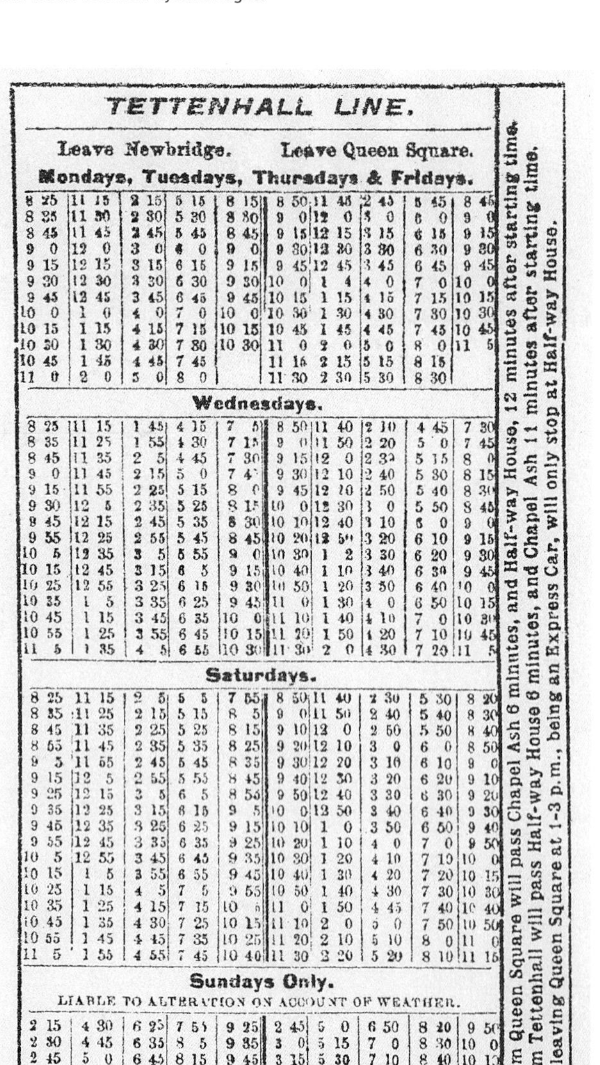

TETTENHALL LINE.

Leave Newbridge.					Leave Queen Square.				
Mondays, Tuesdays, Thursdays & Fridays.									
8 25	11 15	2 15	5 15	8 15	8 50	11 45	2 45	5 45	8 45
8 35	11 30	2 30	5 30	8 30	9 0	12 0	3 0	6 0	9 0
8 45	11 45	2 45	5 45	8 45	9 15	12 15	3 15	6 15	9 15
9 0	12 0	3 0	6 0	9 0	9 30	12 30	3 30	6 30	9 30
9 15	12 15	3 15	6 15	9 15	9 45	12 45	3 45	6 45	9 45
9 30	12 30	3 30	6 30	9 30	10 0	1 4	4 0	7 0	10 0
9 45	12 45	3 45	6 45	9 45	10 15	1 15	4 15	7 15	10 15
10 0	1 0	4 0	7 0	10 0	10 30	1 30	4 30	7 30	10 30
10 15	1 15	4 15	7 15	10 15	10 45	1 45	4 45	7 45	10 45
10 30	1 30	4 30	7 30	10 30	11 0	2 0	5 0	8 0	11 5
10 45	1 45	4 45	7 45		11 16	2 15	5 15	8 15	
11 0	2 0	5 0	8 0		11 30	2 30	5 30	8 30	
Wednesdays.									
8 25	11 15	1 45	4 15	7 5	8 50	11 40	2 10	4 45	7 30
8 35	11 25	1 55	4 30	7 15	9 0	11 50	2 20	5 0	7 45
8 45	11 35	2 5	4 45	7 30	9 15	12 0	2 30	5 15	8 0
9 0	11 45	2 15	5 0	7 45	9 30	12 10	2 40	5 30	8 15
9 15	11 55	2 25	5 15	8 0	9 45	12 20	2 50	5 40	8 30
9 30	12 5	2 35	5 25	8 15	10 0	12 30	3 0	5 50	8 45
9 45	12 15	2 45	5 35	8 30	10 10	12 40	3 10	6 0	9 0
9 55	12 25	2 55	5 45	8 45	10 20	12 50	3 20	6 10	9 15
10 5	12 35	3 5	5 55	9 0	10 30	1 2	3 30	6 20	9 30
10 15	12 45	3 15	6 5	9 15	10 40	1 10	3 40	6 30	9 45
10 25	12 55	3 25	6 15	9 30	10 50	1 20	3 50	6 40	10 0
10 35	1 5	3 35	6 25	9 45	11 0	1 30	4 0	6 50	10 15
10 45	1 15	3 45	6 35	10 0	11 10	1 40	4 10	7 0	10 30
10 55	1 25	3 55	6 45	10 15	11 20	1 50	4 20	7 10	10 45
11 5	1 35	4 5	6 55	10 30	11 30	2 0	4 30	7 20	11 5
Saturdays.									
8 25	11 15	2 5	5 5	7 55	8 50	11 40	2 30	5 30	8 20
8 35	11 25	2 15	5 15	8 5	9 0	11 50	2 40	5 40	8 30
8 45	11 35	2 25	5 25	8 15	9 10	12 0	2 50	5 50	8 40
8 55	11 45	2 35	5 35	8 25	9 20	12 10	3 0	6 0	8 50
9 5	11 55	2 45	5 45	8 35	9 30	12 20	3 10	6 10	9 0
9 15	12 5	2 55	5 55	8 45	9 40	12 30	3 20	6 20	9 10
9 25	12 15	3 5	6 5	8 55	9 50	12 40	3 30	6 30	9 20
9 35	12 25	3 15	6 15	9 5	10 0	12 50	3 40	6 40	9 30
9 45	12 35	3 25	6 25	9 15	10 10	1 0	3 50	6 50	9 40
9 55	12 45	3 35	6 35	9 25	10 20	1 10	4 0	7 0	9 50
10 5	12 55	3 45	6 45	9 35	10 30	1 20	4 10	7 10	10 0
10 15	1 5	3 55	6 55	9 45	10 40	1 30	4 20	7 20	10 15
10 25	1 15	4 5	7 5	9 55	10 50	1 40	4 30	7 30	10 30
10 35	1 25	4 15	7 15	10 5	11 0	1 50	4 45	7 40	10 40
10 45	1 35	4 30	7 25	10 15	11 10	2 0	5 0	7 50	10 50
10 55	1 45	4 45	7 35	10 25	11 20	2 10	5 10	8 0	11 0
11 5	1 55	4 55	7 45	10 40	11 30	2 20	5 20	8 10	11 15
Sundays Only. LIABLE TO ALTERATION ON ACCOUNT OF WEATHER.									
2 15	4 30	6 25	7 55	9 25	2 45	5 0	6 50	8 20	9 50
2 30	4 45	6 35	8 5	9 35	3 0	5 15	7 0	8 30	10 0
2 45	5 0	6 45	8 15	9 45	3 15	5 30	7 10	8 40	10 10
3 0	5 15	6 55	8 25	9 55	3 30	5 45	7 20	8 50	10 20
3 15	5 30	7 5	8 35	10 5	3 45	6 0	7 30	9 0	10 30
3 30	5 45	7 15	8 45	10 15	4 0	6 10	7 40	9 10	10 40
3 45	5 55	7 25	8 55		4 15	6 20	7 50	9 20	
4 0	6 5	7 35	9 5		4 30	6 30	8 0	9 30	
4 15	6 15	7 45	9 15		4 45	6 40	8 10	9 40	

Cars from Queen Square will pass Chapel Ash 6 minutes, and Half-way House, 12 minutes after starting time.
Cars from Tettenhall will pass Half-way House 6 minutes, and Chapel Ash 11 minutes after starting time.
The Car leaving Queen Square at 1-3 p.m., being an Express Car, will only stop at Half-way House.

Horse tram timetable for May 1879. Author's collection

began, by way of Fighting Cocks and Sedgley. The line commenced alongside the Roman Catholic Church in Snow Hill, adjacent to Temple Street, and was unusual in its use of centre grooved rails, also laid to a gauge of 4ft 8½in. The offices and depot were located mid way between Sedgley and Upper Gornal, adjacent to what is now Valley Road. The service, every 75 minutes, took 60 minutes to travel from Wolverhampton through to Dudley.

Both companies had desired to use steam haulage from the outset, but local opposition had restricted them to horsepower. The Wolverhampton Tramways Company, however, reasserted its wish and the council then granted their request, being covered by the Wolverhampton Tramways (Mechanical Power) Order 1880, giving the company power to operate their lines by steam or other mechanical means, subject to council approval, in this instance being granted for steam only on the Tettenhall Road service for an experimental period of six months.

The steam tram arrived at the end of 1880, being hired in from Henry Hughes & Co of Loughborough, and was taken to Newbridge depot on arrival on 24 December. The 6¾-ton four-coupled engine was put through a number of trials during January 1881 and the proposed operation given a Board of Trade inspection by General Hutchinson RE on 28 January. Work required as a result of the inspection did not allow the tram to enter service until 17 May 1881 and included provision of a run-round loop in Queen Square and the conversion of two double-deck horse cars, complete with brakes that could be operated from the steam tram.

The service proved popular with the public, reducing the existing 20-minute journey time to just 13 minutes, and though successful in operation, continuing opposition from some residents along the route, in what was effectively an upper-class district, resulted in the Council refusing to grant the Tramways Company a continuation of the trial period and operation by steam haulage finished on 2 November 1881, never to return,

Dudley, Sedgley & Wolverhampton Tramways Co., Limited,

11, Queen Victoria Street,

London, E.C.,

March 1st, 1882.

Sir,

I beg to inform you that the Certificate for your now fully paid shares is ready, and will be forwarded to you on receipt of your present Certificate and Bankers' Receipts for calls paid.

I remain,

Your obedient Servant,

GEORGE L. MORTON,

Secretary.

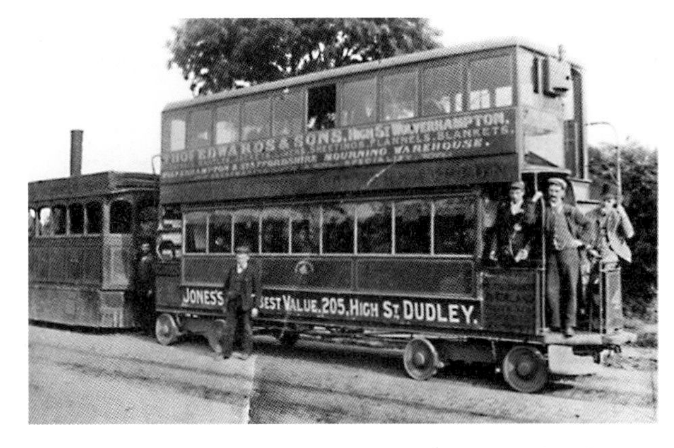

Above: Kitson loco 3 and Starbuck trailer 4 at Springhead passing loop, between Fighting Cocks and Sedgley, in the late 1890s.

Left: Dudley, Sedgley and Wolverhampton Tramways Company, share issue letter.

Below, left: An aerial view of a Steam tram at the Bull Ring in Sedgley.

Below: Tram loco 2 and trailer 4 in Dudley Street, Sedgley, in 1885; the spire of All Saints' Church can be seen in the background. Images: Author's collection

despite a petition presented to the council and signed by over 2,300 members of the general public.

It was proving to be impractical to continue with horse-drawn cars on the undulating and steeply-graded DS&W route between Dudley and Wolverhampton and by 1884 an order had finally been authorised, allowing them to use steam traction, with the council imposing a maximum speed of 8mph when operating within the Borough Boundary. The horse-drawn services ceased on 8 November 1885 while upgrading of the track took place. Orders were placed for the new stock and five horizontal-boilered tram engines were provided by Kitsons. They were fitted with roof-mounted condensers, the Board of Trade requiring that engines consume their own exhaust. For passengers, five double-deck bogie trailer cars were purchased from Starbuck & Company. Operation began along the full length of the line between Snow Hill and Dudley from 16 January 1886, with the 8½-ton steam trams reducing the travelling time to Dudley to 40 minutes. The line had a troubled career, with a winding-up order being obtained in 1887, liquidating shortly afterwards in March 1888.

The operation was sold on 18 October 1888 to the newly-formed Midland Tramways Company Limited, incorporated on 8 December 1888. The new owners reduced the service to an hourly frequency, but the line continued to be beset by financial problems. They in turn liquidated and re-formed as the Dudley and Wolverhampton Tramways Company Limited, incorporated on 24 August 1893. By 1897, there were nine steam engines and five passenger cars operating on the Dudley route, Kitson had supplied one more loco with three coming from Black Hawthorn. The company was to fare no better and again the line went into voluntary liquidation, in 1899.

Bayswater tram in 1861

Sampson Tharne's horse-drawn omnibus 'Wulfruna' on the Penn Road at the junction with The Avenue.

Queen Square in 1866

Newbridge terminus

Queen Square in 1897 with horse tram departing for Newbridge. St Mark's church can be seen in the distance at the bottom of Darlington Street.

Author's collection

CHAPTER 3 WDET Services - Amalgamation and Electrification

On 22 April 1899 the former D&WTC was purchased from the receivers by the British Electric Traction Company Ltd (BET) which were acquiring tramway operators across the Black Country. First registered in 1895 under the name of British Electric Traction (Pioneer) Company Limited, and subsequently changed to British Electric Traction Company Limited, they desired to set about the complete reconstruction of the D&WTC track to 3ft 6in-gauge and electrification of the line, under the Dudley and Wolverhampton Tramways Order of 1899. Wolverhampton Corporation objected to some of the alterations within the proposed order as it included sections of track within the borough where the corporation's option to purchase would fall due in August 1901 under the Wolverhampton Tramways Act of 1899.

The order was amended to exclude the contentious sections within the borough whilst still giving the corporation the option to purchase them within two months of the D&WT Order confirmation. On 20 September 1899, notice was served by the corporation on the BET, instructing them to proceed with the sale of lines within the borough, but as neither party could agree on a price, the sale went to arbitration; a purchase price of £4,250 was eventually agreed with take-over finally being effected on 1 May 1900.

The overhead-electrified stretch between Dudley and Sedgley, now re-gauged to 3ft 6in, was re-opened on 3 October 1900. On 1 February 1901, the BET vested the line in the name of the Wolverhampton District Electric Tramways (WDET), incorporated on 17 December 1900. Cars from the Dudley, Stourbridge & District Electric Tramways Company, also part of the BET group, initially worked the line from Dudley to Sedgley. The line between Sedgley and Fighting Cocks (up to the corporation boundary) remained steam-worked until electrification on 9 January 1902, electric trams then running from Dudley to an end-on junction with Wolverhampton Corporation trams at Fighting Cocks. Full control of the Dudley to Fighting Cocks line was finally transferred to the WDET on 27 October 1903.

Meanwhile, on 1 May 1900 the BET acquired that

Tramcar Service **WILLENHALL, BILSTON, DARLASTON ROUTE.**

MONDAYS (am … pm)

Willenhall	dep	—	—	—	—	--	618	638	then	758	8 8	818	828	838	then	—	158	—	218	then	828	838	848	858	then	1018	1038	1058
Bilston	dep	5 6	530	550	610	—	630	650	every	810	820	830	840	850	every	2 0	210	220	230	every	840	850	9 0	910	every	1030	1050	1110
Darlaston	arr	518	545	6 4	624	—	644	7 3	10	823	833	843	853	9 4	20	213	223	233	243	10	853	9 4	—	924	20	1044	11 4	—
Darlaston	dep	518	545	612	632	—	652	7 3	mins	823	823	843	853	912	mins	213	223	233	243	mins	853	912	—	932	mins	1052	11 5	--
Bilston	dep	530	6 6	626	646	656	7 6	716	until	836	846	9 6	9 6	926	until	226	236	246	256	until	9 6	926	—	946	until	11 6	1117	—
Willenhall	arr	—	618	638	658	7 8	718	728		—	858	918	—	938		238	248	258	3 8		—	938	—	958		—	—	—

TUESDAYS TO FRIDAYS (am … pm)

Willenhall	...	dep		then	3 58	—	4 18	—	4 38	then	6 58	7 8	7 18	7 28	7 38	then	1018	1038	1058
Bilston	...	dep	as	every	4 10	4 20	4 30	4 40	4 50	every	7 10	7 20	7 30	7 40	7 50	every	1030	1050	1110
Darlaston	...	arr	above	20	4 23	4 33	4 43	4 53	5 3	10	7 23	7 32	7 44	—	8 4	20	1044	11 4	—
Darlaston	...	dep	until	mins	4 23	4 33	4 43	4 53	5 3	mins	7 23	7 32	7 52	—	8 12	mins	1052	11 5	—
Bilston	...	dep	8 38	until	4 36	4 46	4 56	5 6	5 16	until	7 36	7 46	8 6	—	8 26	until	11 6	1117	—
Willenhall	..	arr			4 48	4 58	5 8	5 18	5 28		—	7 58	8 18	—	8 38		—	—	—

SATURDAYS (am … pm)

Willenhall	...	dep		then	10 58	—	11 18	11 38	—	11 58	then	10 28	10 38	10 48	10 58	11 12
Bilston	...	dep	as	every	11 10	—	11 30	11 50	12 0	12 10	every	10 40	10 50	11 0	11 10	11 24
Darlaston	...	arr	above	20	11 24	—	11 44	12 3	12 13	12 23	10	10 53	11 3	11 13	—	—
Darlaston	...	dep	until	mins	11 32	—	11 52	12 3	12 13	12 23	mins	10 53	11 3	11 13	—	—
Bilston	...	dep	8 38	until	11 46	11 56	12 6	12 16	12 26	12 36	until	11 6	11 16	11 26	—	—
Willenhall	...	arr			11 58	12 8	12 18	12 28	12 38	12 48		—	—	—	—	—

SUNDAYS (am … pm)

Willenhall	...	dep	—	—	—	9 58	then	5 18	—	5 38	6 0	then	10 15	10 30	10 45	11 0
Bilston	...	dep	9 10	9 30	9 50	1010	every	5 30	5 45	6 0	6 15	every	10 30	10 50	11 0	11 12
Darlaston	...	arr	9 24	9 44	10 4	1024	20	5 44	5 59	6 14	6 29	15	10 44	11 4	—	—
Darlaston	...	dep	9 32	9 52	1012	1032	mins	5 45	6 0	6 15	6 30	mins	10 45	11 5	—	—
Bilston	...	dep	9 46	10 6	1026	1046	until	6 0	6 15	6 30	6 45	until	11 0	11 17	—	—
Willenhall	...	arr	9 58	1018	1038	1058		6 15	6 30	6 45	7 0		—	—	—	—

FARES

	Single	Child		Single	Child
Willenhall to Old Football	} 1½d.	1d.	Loxdale Street to Moxley	1d.	1d.
Davis Loop to Bilston Town Hall ...			Moxley to Darlaston Bull Stake	1d.	½d.
Willenhall to Bilston Town Hall	2d.	1d.	Bilston Town Hall to Moxley	} 1½d.	1d.
Old Football Ground to Bilston Town Hall	} 1d.	1d.	Loxdale Street to Darlaston Bull Stake ...		
Bilston Town Hall to Loxdale Street ...			Bilston Town Hall to Darlaston Bull Stake ...	2d.	1d.

BET timetable for Willenhall to Darlaston. Author's collection

part of the Wolverhampton Tramways Company horse-worked line that lay outside the Wolverhampton town boundary, under the name of Bilston & District Tramways. On 1 February 1901, the assets of the Bilston & District Tramways were transferred to the WDET, with conversion of the track to the Black Country standard gauge of 3ft 6in. By 15 July an extension to the line was operating to Fighting Cocks. This had been obtained under the South Staffordshire Light Railway Order 1900, running rights having already been obtained over the South Staffordshire between Moxley and Darlaston. The intention was to link up all the isolated ends of lines then under their control, and an extension order in 1900 covered lines from Bilston to Bradley and Bilston to Willenhall, to connect with the isolated stretch of line from Deans Road to Willenhall now also owned by the BET.

Electric services commenced on 14 July 1902 from the corporation boundary at Stow Heath Lane to Moxley, via Bilston and from Bilston to Fighting Cocks, with a west to south spur physically connecting to the Dudley line at Fighting Cocks (a feature that was carried into trolleybus working, remaining until withdrawal of the route to Bilston), and from Bilston to Willenhall on 15 July 1902, terminating at the Market Place, destined in the future to see tram services from Wolverhampton and Walsall.

1902 would also see further WDET electric services commencing: Willenhall to Deans Road on 6 November, where it met the corporation tram service from Wolverhampton, (working on the Lorain system) and Willenhall to Darlaston on 6 December, extended to the Bull Stake on 15 December. The initial stock needed to work the new WDET electrified lines came from the Electric Railway and Tramway Carriage Works of Preston and consisted of 13 double-deck open-top cars in the standard BET livery of mustard and ivory; this went through a number of changes, eventually becoming green and cream. More expansion came on 23 April 1903 when running powers were granted

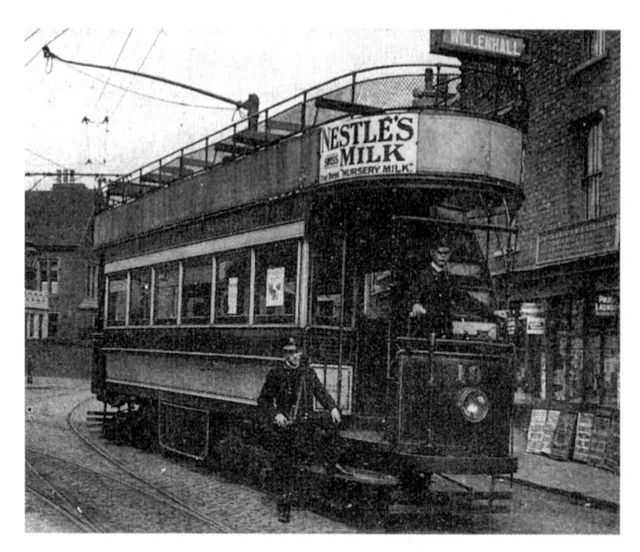

Willenhall-bound tram at Darlaston Author's collection

over the South Staffordshire Tramways Company tracks and WDET cars from Bilston were able to run through from Moxley to Darlaston.

Meanwhile, back in Wolverhampton the corporation had been busy and decided to exercise their right, enshrined in the Wolverhampton Tramways Order of 1877, to purchase the Wolverhampton Tramways Company after 21 years of operation, with notice being served on 6 October 1898 requiring the Wolverhampton Tramways Company to sell all parts of their business that lay within the borough. The BET was aggressively trying to enter corporation territory and had for some time past been trying by various means to purchase the tramway, suggesting in 1896 that the corporation purchase the line and then re-sell to the BET at the same price; this being followed in May 1897 by the proposal that the BET purchase both this line and the D&WTC, transferring them both to a new operating company called the Wolverhampton and District Electric Tramways Company. As might be expected, Wolverhampton Corporation, determined to keep the BET out of what it saw as sacrosanct territory, rejected both proposals outright, also taking exception to the suggested new name, on the grounds that it could imply some measure of ownership or control by the corporation to members of the general public.

After some hard negotiating, including the use of a Board of Trade arbitrator, a purchase price of £22,500 was agreed, the corporation acquiring all lines in the town centre and the route outright to Newbridge, the Bilston route as far as Ettingshall Road plus one rail to Stow Heath Lane (the borough boundary running down the centre of the road) and the Willenhall route as far as Coventry Street, plus one rail again from there to Deans Road. At the same time, the BET took over the lines from Stow Heath Lane to Bilston, the Moxley extension and Deans Road to Willenhall, a mutual agreement not to encroach on each other's territory being written into the sale.

Purchase was completed on 1 May 1900 and on this date the first official horse tram to be operated by the newly-formed Wolverhampton Corporation Tramways Department left Queen Square at 7.40 a.m., bound for Tettenhall, the old Wolverhampton Tramways Co Ltd being wound up on 15 March 1901. It was intended that the purchases would be made with a view to narrowing the gauge to 3ft 6in in the fullness of time, and electrifying the lines.

The stock acquired for this enterprise comprised seventeen horse-drawn trams and seventy-five horses to operate them, all coming from the Wolverhampton Tramways Company. Also included in the purchase were the two depots plus the General Manager and most of his forty-five staff. Upon investigation, five of the trams were declared unfit for further use and scrapped. Subsequent purchases were made to supplement the fleet and included three trams at £60 each from the North Metropolitan Tramways Company, in a yellow livery, which was retained, as were their existing fleet numbers 285/286 and 288.

BET car 2 at Fighting Cocks in 1900 with driver H Gough. It is on the long Bilston, Sedgley and Dudley route. The short lifeguard would indicate that it is not dual fitted for Lorain operation. Author's collection

Purchases from Liverpool Corporation in 1901 included 12 open-top horse buses that also retained their livery and numbers, being 19/31/37/39/95/103/115/118/130/132/136 and 142. They were to be put to good use as a stopgap measure until eventual conversion to electric traction took place. By 1904, all horse-drawn vehicles had been withdrawn from service.

Following on from the Wolverhampton Tramways Act of 1899, the BET continued to work their variously acquired tramways themselves for some months before making an operational transfer on 1 February 1901 to the WDET, with the D&WTC being wound up on 27 January 1902.

South Staffordshire car 17 at Darlaston in 1929, with a service for Wednesbury.

Darlaston Bull Ring. Note the overhead wiring layout.

Church Street, Bilston in 1910

Dudley and Stourbridge steam tram

Kings Hill Wednesbury

Birmingham and Midland Tramways steam tram conductor

Author's collection

CHAPTER 4 | WDET & Other Histories

Wolverhampton District Electric Tramways Company Limited
Dudley, Sedgley & Wolverhampton Tramways Company Limited
Midland Tramway Company Limited
Dudley & Wolverhampton Tramways Company Limited
1883-1928

The origins of the WDET lie in a six-mile line constructed originally to the railway standard gauge of 4ft 8½in, between Dudley and Wolverhampton, via Sedgley. Authorised under the Dudley, Sedgley & Wolverhampton Tramways Order of 1880, the line opened to the public on 7 May 1883. It was horse-worked from the start, and it quickly became obvious that this form of traction would not be suitable for the hilly and undulating nature of the route. Application was made to use steam traction, and this was granted by 1884, with the proviso of a maximum speed of 8mph being observed within the Wolverhampton borough boundary. After reconstruction of the track to take the heavier weights involved, services were resumed on 16 January 1886, with Kitson steam locos hauling trailer cars supplied by Starbuck. This ill-starred and poorly-managed company continued to have more than its share of troubles, financial problems causing it to go into liquidation in 1888. Sold to the Midland Tramways Company on 18 October, it fared no better, liquidating and re-forming as the Dudley & Wolverhampton Tramways Company in 1893.

In 1899 the tramway again went into voluntary liquidation, this time being rescued by the British Electric Traction Company (BET), who purchased the concern from the receivers on 22 April. They immediately proceeded to reconstruct the entire line, reducing the track gauge to the Black Country standard of 3ft 6in, and under the Wolverhampton Tramways Order of 1899, electrify the system. The Order also gave Wolverhampton Corporation the right to purchase track within its boundary, with completion of this purchase being effected on 1 May 1900 after much wrangling over the purchase price, with the transaction finally going to arbitration.

The Dudley to Sedgley section opened on 3 October 1900, with that between Sedgley and the Wolverhampton boundary at Fighting Cocks following suit on 9 January 1902. The BET was adept at moving trams around from its various concerns as required and initially electric cars borrowed from the Dudley, Stourbridge & District Tramways Company worked the Dudley to Sedgley section, the line between Sedgley and Fighting Cocks remaining steam-worked until conversion was complete in 1902.

On 17 December 1900, the Wolverhampton District Electric Tramways Company Limited came into being when it was registered to purchase the assets of the Bilston & District Tramways Company Limited from the BET; the Bilston tramway was part of the division of tracks acquired from Wolverhampton by the BET, under the 1899 Tramways Order, the intention being to combine it with the Dudley line under a new BET-owned operating company. It had originally been part of the 1878 Wolverhampton Tramways Company standard-gauge horse tramway. The Dudley line was vested in the new company on 1 February 1901.

Further electrified extensions to the 3ft 6in system were put in place to link up isolated sections and electric working started as follows –

14 July 1902, Stow Heath Lane to Moxley via Bilston.
14 July 1902, Bilston to Fighting Cocks, with a spur on to the Dudley line.
15 July 1902, Bilston to Willenhall, terminating at the Market Place.
August 1902, Bilston to Bradley.
6 November 1902, Willenhall to Deans Road, where it met the Lorain-operated trams from Wolverhampton on route 5.
6 December 1902, Willenhall to Darlaston, extended to the Bull Stake in the centre of town on 15 December.

The rolling stock to start services was provided in the form of 13 double-deck open-top 4-wheel cars, supplied by the Electric Railway and Tramway Carriage Works, of Preston, supplied in the BET livery of mustard and ivory; this was subsequently changed to lake and cream, finally finishing up as green and cream.

By use of running powers over the South Staffordshire Tramways track, services were extended from Moxley to Darlaston with through working by WDET trams, from 23 April 1903. Full control of the Dudley line was passed to the new company on 27 October 1903. In a further political twist, Wolverhampton Corporation trams were seen working through from Stow Heath Lane to Bilston from 9 November 1905, and Deans Road to Willenhall from 18 April 1906. This was made possible by fitting a number of cars with overhead collection equipment, using nearside trolley poles. Similarly, some BET cars were dual-equipped with Lorain equipment, though these trams did not enter service on the Dudley route until 15 October 1906.

With the collapse of the South Staffordshire Tramways empire on 1 April 1924, the WDET took over operation of all services between Wednesbury and Darlaston. They also took over joint working with Walsall Corporation of routes from that town to Wednesbury and Darlaston. On 1 October 1925 Walsall Corporation acquired the line between Willenhall and Darlaston, and on 31 August 1928, with the exception of the former South Staffordshire routes, which were transferred to the Dudley, Stourbridge & District Company, Wolverhampton Corporation purchased all the remaining WDET assets, effectively closing the Company.

Fleet No	Into Service	Type	Builder	Truck	Seating
Horse Cars					
1-7	1883	D/Deck	Ashbury	Unknown	Unknown
Steam Locos					
1-5	1885	4-wheel	Kitson		
6	1894	4-wheel	Black Hawthorn		
7-9	1898	4-wheel	Black Hawthorn		
Trailer Cars					
1-5	1885	D/Deck Top-covered Bogie	Starbuck		Unknown

N.B. – Steam locos 6, 8-9 were ex Huddersfield Corporation, new to them 1885/6. All horse cars were withdrawn by 1885. Steam locos and trailer cars were withdrawn and scrapped by 1902.

Fleet No	Into Service	Type	Builder	Truck	Seating
Electric Tramcars					
1-13	1901	D/Deck Open-top 4-wheel	ERTCW	Brill 21E	22/22
14-30	1902	D/Deck Open-top Bogie	Brush	Brush	36/34
1-4	1904	D/Deck Open-top Bogie	Brush	Brush	34/30
31-32	1908	D/Deck Open-top 4-wheel	ERTCW	Brill 21E	22/22
33	1914	D/Deck Open-top 4-wheel	Brush	Brush	26/22
34	1923	D/Deck Open-top 4-wheel	Brush	Brush	26/22
18	1924	D/Deck Top-covered 4-wheel	Brush	Brush L&C Radial	26/22
33	1925	D/Deck Open-top 4-wheel	ERTCW	Brill 21E	22/22

NOTE ON TRAMCARS

Nos 1-13. (1901 group). Fitted with direct staircases. These trams were later canopied. Nos 1-4 went to Dudley, Stourbridge & District c.1904.

Nos 1-4. (1904 group). These were ex Stourbridge & District Electric Traction, new in 1901 and their numbers 39-42, subsequently rebuilt, to single deck c.1914.

Nos 14-30. A number of cars (unknown) plus No 18, were reduced to single deck c.1914.

No 18. (1924 group). This was an ex-South Staffordshire Tramways car, their number 34 and new to them in 1904.

Nos 31-32. Ex-Dudley, Stourbridge & District Electric Traction cars of 1904.

No 33. (1914 group). Ex-Birmingham & Midland Tramways car, new to them in 1904.

No 33. (1925 group). Ex-Dudley, Stourbridge & District Electric Traction car, their number 41.

Corporation car 19 is seen at Bilston Town Hall after the introduction of through running.

Wellington Road, Bilston, around 1907 at the junction with Mount Pleasant. A Wolverhampton-bound tramcar can be seen in the distance.

Images Cliff Brown collection courtesy John Hughes

Cobble setts being re-laid in Millfields Road, Ettingshall during 1926. The LMS railway station Ettingshall Road & Bilston is in the background. Cliff Brown collection courtesy John Hughes

Sedgley Bull Ring with trams to and from Dudley at the passing loop. Author's collection

High Street, Bilston, circa 1910.

The WDET depot building in Mount Pleasant, Bilston. The wiring layout, which can just be glimpsed to the right, would suggest that this picture was taken in later trolleybus days.

Road repairs on Ettingshall Road in 1970, near Millfields Road, revealed the old tram tracks, buried under the tarmac for over 40 years. The view is looking towards Ettingshall.

The Bull Stake at Darlaston.

WDET car 19 at Stow Heath terminus, prior to 1905.

Bilston Road, at Stow Heath Lane junction, effectively the end of the Corporation tramway lines. At this point, through passengers would have to change to a car of the WDET system; one can be seen waiting in the distance. Author's collection

A Wolverhampton Corporation tram waits at the Fighting Cocks crossroads, as a WDET tram from Bilston stops on the curve out of Parkfield Road into Dudley Road. Author's collection

Dudley, Stourbridge & District Electric Traction Company Limited
Dudley & Stourbridge Steam Tramways Company Limited
1884-1930

Originally registered on 22 December 1880 under the title of the Dudley, Stourbridge & Kingswinford Tramways Company Ltd, and subsequently authorised under the Order of 1881, the tramway opened on 21 May 1884 and was operated by the Dudley & Stourbridge Steam Tramways Company Ltd, using a track gauge of 3ft 6in. The line ran from Dudley station, then under the control of the London & North Western Railway, by way of Brierley Hill and Amblecote, to Stourbridge. The proposed branch to Kingswinford was not authorised and dispensed with. Steam-hauled from the outset, the company were supplied with eight locos from Kitson and eight double-deck trailer cars built by Starbuck; four more Kitson engines were to arrive between 1885 and1896.

The BET purchased a controlling interest in the operation on 2 April 1898, and immediately started upon electrification of the system, changing the name in the process to the Dudley, Stourbridge & District Electric Traction Company Ltd. July 1899 saw conversion completed and the system ready for use, with the first 18 single-deck electric cars arriving from Brush; the standard BET livery of mustard and ivory was applied to these cars. Full operation commenced on 26 July. The remaining steam trams were then rapidly withdrawn.

In 1900, two branches were opened, the first one on 19 October running some three miles from Dudley to Cradley Heath, via Blowers Green, Netherton and Old Hill. This was followed on 7 December by a line to Kingswinford, finally opened some 10 years after the idea was put forward. Further extensions were constructed, from Stourbridge to Lye on 1 November 1902, Stourbridge to Wollaston Junction on 13 December, where it connected with the Kinver Light Railway at the Fish Inn, and Old Hill to Blackheath on 19 December 1904. On 29 September 1902 the company purchased a controlling interest in the Kinver Light Railway, which it had worked on their behalf, since first opening on 5 April 1901, the purchase adding a further four miles to the tramway system.

April 1924 saw a further acquisition when the company took over operation of the South Staffordshire Tramway Company's route from Dudley to Wednesbury: the SSTC had to vacate the depot at Tividale and operation in the West Bromwich area, due to the expiry of the lease. This in turn proved to be the cause of much of the BET's subsequent undoing in the Black Country, leaving a large hole in the network that was rapidly filled by encroaching bus operators as they sensed a foothold. The ripple effect then spread with several closures being effected in quick succession. Dudley to Kingswinford on 11 April 1926, followed later that year by the lines from Stourbridge to both Kingswinford and Wollaston. Old Hill to Blackheath and Stourbridge to Lye both followed in 1927 with Dudley to Cradley Heath ending in 1929. The system finally closed on 1 March 1930, with the withdrawal of the remaining two tramway services from Dudley to Wednesbury and Stourbridge. With the closure, the last BET operating company ceased to exist.

Fleet No	Into Service	Type	Builder	Truck	Seating
Steam Locos					
1-8	1884	4-wheel	Kitson		
9	1885	4-wheel	Kitson		
10	1891	4-wheel	Kitson		
11	1895	4-wheel	Kitson		
12	1896	4-wheel	Kitson		
Trailer Cars					
1-8	1884	D/Deck Canopy-top Bogie	Starbuck		32/30

N.B. – On withdrawal in 1900, eight steam trams saw further use, with 1, 2, 5 and 8-12 being transferred to the Birmingham & Midland Tramways Company Ltd, being allocated numbers 34, 1, 31, 33, 32,10, 30 and 29 respectively.

Fleet No	Into Service	Type	Builder	Truck	Seating
Electric Tramcars					
1-18	1899	S/Deck Combination 4-wheel	Brush	Peckham	28 (6+16+6)
19-22	1900	S/Deck 4-wheel	ERTCW	Lord Baltimore	26
23-38	1901	D/Deck Open-top 4-wheel	ERTCW	Brill 21E	26/22
39-42	1901	D/Deck Open-top Bogie	Brush	Brush	34/30
43-45	1901	S/Deck 4-wheel	ERTCW	Lord Baltimore	26
46-48	1901	D/Deck Open-top Bogie	ERTCW	Brill 22E	Unknown
49-51	1902	S/Deck Combination Toastrack Bogie	Brush	Brush	56 (12+32+12)
52-59	1902	S/Deck Combination Bogie	Brush	Brush D	52 (10+32+10)
39-42	1904	D/Deck Open-top 4-wheel	ERTCW	Brill 21E	22/22
61-62	1910	S/Deck Combination 4-wheel	City of Birmingham Tramways	Brush L&C Radial	34 (6+22+6)
63-68	1910	S/Deck Roofed Toastrack 4-wheel	City of Birmingham Tramways	Brush L&C Radial	40
46-47	1912	S/Deck Bogie	Brush	Brush	Unknown
60	1913	D/Deck Open-top 4-wheel	Birmingham & Midland JTC	Birmingham & Midland JTC	26/22
69	1913	D/Deck Open-top	Birmingham & Midland JTC	Birmingham & Midland JTC	26/22

Fleet No	Into Service	Type	Builder	Truck	Seating
1	1915	S/Deck Combination 4-wheel	Birmingham & Midland JTC	Birmingham & Midland JTC	32 (16+16)
2	1915	S/Deck Combination 4-wheel	Birmingham & Midland	Birmingham & Midland	32 (16+16)
7	1915	S/Deck Combination 4-wheel	Birmingham & Midland	Birmingham & Midland	32 (16+16)
10	1915	S/Deck Combination 4-wheel	Birmingham & Midland	Birmingham & Midland	32 (16+16)
6	1915	S/Deck Semi-open Combination Bogie	Birmingham & Midland JTC	Brush D	56 (16+24+16)
21	1916	S/Deck Semi-open Combination Bogie	Birmingham & Midland JTC	Brush D	56 (16+24+16)
32	1916	S/Deck Semi-open Combination	Birmingham & Midland JTC	Brush D	56 (16+24+16)
70	1916	S/Deck Semi-open Combination Bogie	Birmingham & Midland JTC	Brush D	56 (16+24+16)

NOTES ON TRAMCARS

Nos 23-28. Five of these cars (numbers uncertain) were transferred to the South Staffordshire Tramways Co. Ltd. c.1911 and renumbered 2, 32, 33, 35 and 38.

Nos 39-42 (1901 group). Fitted with reversed staircases. Withdrawn c.1904 and transferred to Wolverhampton District Tramways (re-numbered 1-4).

Nos 39-42. Ex Wolverhampton District 1-4 (new to them in 1901).

Nos 43-45. These were placed on temporary loan to the Kinver Light Railway, in April 1901, taking Nos 1-3.

Nos 46-48. Loaned from the Kinver Light Railway in 1901 and converted to 38-seat single-deck cars during their stay, they were later returned to their original base, after purchase of the Kinver line, retaining their DS&D numbers, being more suitable for operation on the Kinver section in their new form.

Nos 49-51. Ex-Kinver Light Railway trams (new to them in 1901).

Nos 46-47 (1912 group). Ex-South Staffordshire Tramways Co. Ltd. (from the 10-27 double-deck batch in 1902). They were rebuilt to single-deck cars.

Nos 61-62. Ex-Birmingham & Midland Tramways Nos 51-52, and new in 1904.

Nos 63-68. Ex-City of Birmingham Tramways Co. Ltd. Nos 257-262, and new in 1900 as cable cars.

Kinver Light Railway 1901-1930

The village of Kinver lies a short distance outside the industrial Black Country and forms a southern outpost of Staffordshire, bordering on the neighbouring counties of Shropshire and Worcestershire; its existence was first recorded in 736AD as Cynibre, the word meaning 'Great Hill'. What little industrial past Kinver possessed was well and truly over by 1882; prior to the recession, iron had been worked in the area since 1387 and much use had been made of the River Stour and its tributary, with at least five mills operating within the parish in the 17th century.

This line was intended to provide for both the needs of a largely isolated community and to promote the idea of healthy leisure pursuits into the countryside, for those people living in the more populous areas of the industrial Black Country, where clean air and expanses of grassland were relatively rare. Largely rural throughout its length, it ran for 4 miles 15 chains through the pleasant and rural landscape. The line was first promoted by the BET using the Kinver Light Railway Order of 1898 and constructed at a cost of around £27,000. It was an ill-starred start, as virtually every

The Stewponey Inn, with a crowd of holidaymakers. Author's collection

authority whose land the proposed tramway would run through had opposed the construction; this included the sole private landowner and, surprisingly, Kinver Parish Council. However, the public enquiry that was held did much to smooth the way, and with the line of route being altered slightly, the scheme was approved on 7 March 1899, with construction starting almost immediately.

Built to the standard Black Country gauge of 3ft 6in, the first 1 mile 15 chain stretch from Amblecote to The Ridge used grooved street tramway rail, with the remaining 3-mile private right of way stretch making use of wooden-sleepered Vignoles non-grooved rail, the last 1 mile 48 chains of which required no less than a dozen bridges across the canal and river as it entered Kinver. Somewhat unusually, the off-road sections of line used wooden traction poles for the overhead wiring, rather than the conventional metal ones, a methodology shared with the totally unconnected and rather distant Great Northern Railway of Ireland, which had a penchant for economy, using unpainted wooden telegraph poles on which to erect their signals!

With the construction completed by March 1901, a Board of Trade inspection was made on 1 April, and the line opened for business on 5 April 1901, using cars borrowed from the Dudley, Stourbridge and District system. For the opening, three double-deck open-top trams were delivered in 1900 from the Electric Railway and Tramway Carriage Works, of Preston. It had been the intention to use these, but the Board of Trade blocked this idea, citing a risk factor of their instability on the sleepered stretch between the Stewponey Hotel and Ridge Top, on the Stourton to Wollaston section, also imposing a 10mph restriction on this section and insisting that single-deck bogie cars were used. A further constraint placed upon the company was the ban on night-time running, due to the complete lack of signalling at any of the passing loops.

To ensure the opening went ahead, the BET quickly organised the cutting down of three double-deck bogie cars to single-deck, and these were diverted from their DS&D system to cover operations, which proved to be quite convenient all round, as the DS&D were to work the line on behalf of the light railway company. The line was duly opened with much excitement on Friday 5 April 1901, initially operating a half-hourly service at just 3d for the complete journey. Its popularity rapidly grew and an immediate order was placed with Brush, for three additional tramcars. They arrived during 1901, and were of open mid-section, with 'toast rack' seating.

The line started outside the Fish Inn at Amblecote, on the Stourbridge to Wolverhampton road, where it met and physically connected with the tracks of the DS&D. Two depots were constructed: at The Hyde, in Kinver, and at Amblecote, where the line started on its journey via Wollaston; in a throwback to the time of tram operation, the area is still known as Wollaston Junction to this day. From here, the line headed due west via Wollaston Road, and High Street Wollaston, leaving there by way of Bridgnorth Road to The Ridge, where it entered a reserved roadside section, and continued parallel to the main road, until it encountered the landmark of the Stewponey Hotel (since demolished and replaced by luxury apartments).

At this point the line crossed what is now the main A449 Wolverhampton to Kidderminster road, and, joined by the Stourbridge Canal a short distance to the north, it crossed the Staffordshire & Worcestershire Canal on its own independent little bridge, the rusting remains being extant until quite recently. Once over the canal, the line immediately crossed the River Stour by a plate girder bridge, and turning through 90 degrees, continued gently downhill, through pleasant rolling countryside, on its own fenced-off right of way, never straying far from the road leading to Kinver. This section was laid with traditional flat-bottom rails, in the true style of a light railway.

The final approach of the line led to the Hyde meadows, with the line terminating in Mill Lane, Kinver, under the watchful eye of St Peter's of the Rock, the church being high above the terminus on the sandstone cliffs for which Kinver is justifiably famous. The church is dedicated to the memory of the first king of Mercia's two murdered sons, Wulphad and Ruffinus. The terminus was equipped with a waiting room and ticket office. With the basic service being every 30 minutes, Hyde depot came into active use each summer to deal with the extra movements. In addition to the four-road tram depot, capable of holding eight cars, there were extra sidings to cope with tourist traffic generated during the summer months. The tramway was enterprising, operating a goods and parcels service, which was extended to include milk churns and garden produce, initially being carried on the motorman's platform, but later on specially constructed open truck trailers, as business increased, empty milk churns being returned to their pick-up point by other trams later in the day!

A controlling interest in the company was acquired on 29 September 1902 by the DS&D, the line effectively becoming part of their system. The BET group was very good at marketing the use of the Kinver line, coining the phrase Switzerland of the Midlands for the village, in its attempt to improve the usage of its tram service. With increasing requests being made for through working by trams from other parts of the Black Country network, the track was substantially upgraded, and virtually all of the Vignoles rail had been replaced by June 1903, with conventional grooved rail.

Thereafter increasing use was made of the line's potential during the summer seasons with through cars working in from many distant parts of the BET Black Country empire, such as Walsall and Birmingham, and the line's capacity was further maximised by running some cars in pairs, uncoupled, a number of passing loops being extended to accommodate this tactic. It was not unknown to find the occasional double-deck car still slipping down to Kinver, despite the misgivings and sanctions imposed by the Board of Trade, though the regular line services were generally in the hands of the line's own fleet of specially-built and separately-maintained single-deck cars. By 1905, the KLR had joined the BET's Parcels Express Service, an innovative service that was well ahead of its time. It was operated using small, purpose-built box van trams with a capacity of two tons that could carry parcels and general goods, virtually anywhere within the Black Country tramway network.

One of the more unusual loads carried by the tramway was the funeral coffin of the Reverend E G Hexall on 28 January 1915, complete with mourners. Reverend Hexall was a popular figure, with two great passions in life, the well-being of the tramway workers and the welfare of crippled boys. When he moved into the area, he took Hyde House, near Stourton, renaming it Bethany and turning it into a home where the boys were taught a trade and looked after.

He was a deservedly popular figure locally and on the day of his funeral the coffin was carried by tram company employees on a lavishly decorated semi-open hearse, created by adapting one of the open truck trailers. This was attached behind tram 12 (possibly a DS&D car) carrying the mourners, and followed by another tram, filled with those who wished to honour the clergyman and pay their last respects. The second tram involved was 47, which started off in life as a South Staffordshire Tramways double-deck car before being cut down in 1912 to single-deck, for use on the Kinver line. The funeral procession ran from Mill Lane, through to Wordsley, where the service was held in the parish church, the sad event being captured on film with a photograph of the cortege being taken at Darby's Farm passing loop, midway between Stourton and Wollaston.

With the onset of the First World War, the line, in common with other industries, began to suffer from a lack of maintenance. Deterioration set in and tourist traffic all over the country began to fade away. The encroaching motor coach trade steadily ate into what was left, and through workings, one of the main sources of summer traffic, began to dwindle as the BET system contracted, with other tramway companies ceasing operations. Despite the obvious loss that closure would occasion to the local area, the local authorities made no offer of support or financial assistance. Eventually, closure became inevitable and came on 8 February 1930, just a few short weeks before closure of the Dudley and Stourbridge parent system on 1 March 1930. Had the Kinver line survived, its potential as a present-day tourist attraction would have been enormous, as would its capability of taking many thousands of private cars off the roads at weekends.

Inspector Edward Morris with a crew at the Hyde Depot.

A crew pose for the photographer.

Mill Lane terminus.

The Kinver Orchestra at Mill Lane terminus in the 1920s. The multitude of trams at the terminus would suggest a very busy weekend for the company; perhaps an organised outing was also involved.

The funeral tram provided for the Reverend Hexall on 28 January 1915.

Images: Author's collection

Above: This photograph was taken at the Stewponey Hotel on the Wall Heath to Kidderminster road, on 20 April 1965. The picture is looking towards the Stewponey and shows the remains of a bridge over the local brook, once the trackbed of the Kinver Light Railway and still surviving 35 years after closure. The gentleman in the picture is Paul Sutherland, one-time chairman of the National Trolleybus Association.

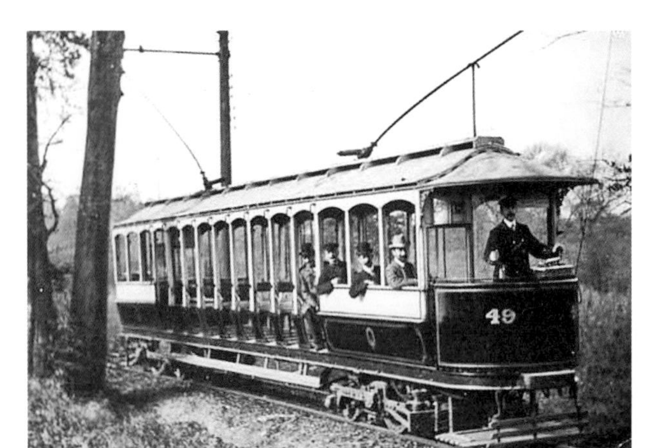

Above: Kinver tram in the open countryside.

Above: The approach to the Stewponey Hotel in August 2008. A traction pole still survives, over 80 years after closure of the system.

Below: The faded green paint can still be seen at the top of the pole. The main road at the back of the picture was once crossed at right angles by the tramway.

Left: Uncovering the still-extant maintenance pits at the Hyde depot in Kinver, on 29 June 1952.

Images: Author's collection

Fleet No	Into Service	Type	Builder	Truck	Seating
Electric Tramcars					
1-3	1900	D/Deck Open-top Bogie	ERTCW	Brill 22E	Unknown
Unknown	1901	S/Deck	ERTCW	Lord Baltimore	26
1-3	1901	S/Deck Open Combination Toastrack	Brush	Brush	56 (12+32+12)
46-48	1902	S/Deck Bogie	ERTCW	Brill 22E	38
63-68	1911	S/Deck Covered Toastrack 4-wheel	City of Birmingham Tramways	Brush L&C	40
46-47	1912	S/Deck Bogie	Brush	Brill 22E	38
6, 21, 32, 70	1916	S/Deck Semi-open Combination Bogie	Birmingham & Midland	Brush D	56 (16+24+16)

NOTES ON TRAMCARS
The Kinver Light Railway was generally maintained with its own dedicated fleet of single-deck tramcars, though they were numbered within the Dudley Stourbridge and District parent company's fleet.

Nos 1-3 (1900 group). These were exchanged for cars from the DS&D system.

Nos 1-3 (1901 group). Re-numbered 49-51 and moved to DS&S fleet in 1902.

Nos 46-48. These were the original numbers 1-3 of 1900. They were converted to single deck cars by the DS&D, and returned to the KLR system in 1902.

Nos 46-47 (1912 group). Ex-South Staffordshire Tramways; former Brush double-deck, open top-cars (numbers unknown). They were cut down to single-deck, receiving the trucks from the earlier numbers 46-47.

Nos 63-68. Previously City of Birmingham Tramways 257-262; former cable cars, converted to electric traction in 1904.

South Staffordshire Tramways Company Limited
South Staffordshire & Birmingham District Steam Tramways Company Limited
1883-1924

Under the Staffordshire Tramways Order of 1879, this 3ft 6in gauge tramway was constructed for the South Staffordshire & Birmingham District Steam Tramways Company, whose system was incorporated on 28 March 1882. The initial service was to start from Handsworth in Birmingham, adjacent to the New Inn, and run to Darlaston, serving West Bromwich and Wednesbury en route. Rolling stock was purchased in the form of 21 steam locos from three different suppliers, Beyer Peacock, Wilkinson and Thomas Green, together with 28 double-deck trailer cars from two well-known suppliers, Starbuck and Falcon. The service opened on 16 July 1883 and the brown and cream-liveried rolling stock was accommodated at the purpose-built Kings Hill depot in Wednesbury.

With the line operating successfully, further expansion quickly followed –

14 January 1884, from Carter's Green in West Bromwich to Great Bridge.
21 January 1884, Darlaston to Moxley.
21 January 1884, Wednesbury to Dudley via Tipton.
4 December 1884, Darlaston to Pleck.
4 December 1884, Wednesbury to Bloxwich, running via Pleck and Walsall; 4 December 1884, a spur in Walsall to Mellish Road.
12 October 1885, Great Bridge to Dudley.
21 November 1885, a short extension to the Bloxwich line.

The company name was changed on 26 August 1889 to the South Staffordshire Tramways Company and shortly after this, a decision was made to electrify the system. With completion of two routes, Bloxwich to Walsall and Darlaston to Walsall (Mellish Road), the new electric service opened on 1 January 1893. The electrified lines were sold to the BET on 11 June 1899 and transferred to a new operating company, the South Staffordshire Tramways Company Limited, this being registered on 21 July 1899. The new company was quick to agree a lease on the remaining steam-worked lines, the agreement taking affect on 1 February 1900, though the official takeover did not occur until 23 June that year.

As a body, town councils were now becoming more proactive and aware of the benefits in having some control over public transport inside their borough.

Accordingly, using the powers available to them, Walsall Corporation decided to acquire all tracks within their boundaries, purchase becoming effective on 1 January 1901. They were then leased back to the company until 31 December 1903, after which time Walsall were in a position to operate their own tramway service.

During 1904, the Birmingham and Midland Tramways Ltd acquired the BET interest in the company, thereby coming under the management of the Birmingham and Midland Tramways Joint Committee. Company trams continued to work up to the Walsall boundary at Pleck, the change of cars needed by through passengers not being appreciated, and so unpopular did it become that as from 1 May 1907, through working was implemented, with corporation and company cars jointly operating over routes from Walsall to Darlaston and Wednesbury. West Bromwich Corporation also acquired tracks within their boundary with effect from 21 January 1902. They were then converted for electric operation and again leased back to the company for 21 years. Handsworth and Wednesbury councils adopted the same tactic, and Dudley Town Council approved a 30-year lease when they purchased tracks in 1909.

Sections of track converted for electric operation opened as follows –

20 December 1902, Handsworth to Carter's Green.
24 January 1903, Carter's Green to Great Bridge.
19 February 1903, Carter's Green to Hill Top (West Bromwich).
10 April 1903, Hill Top to Wednesbury.
23 April 1903, Darlaston to Moxley.
30 May 1903, Great Bridge to Dudley (Railway Station).
8 October 1903, Wednesbury to the 'White Horse' public house in High Street.

The Darlaston to Moxley section was generally worked by trams from the Wolverhampton District Electric Tramways Company as part of their Bilston to Darlaston route, being serviced by Bilston depot. Steam tram working was steadily withdrawn, with the last one running on 15 June 1904, and the final electric section, between Wednesbury and Dudley, commenced working on 22 January 1907. A new through service was initiated on 9 October 1912, running from Colmore Row in Birmingham to Darlaston, via Handsworth, West Bromwich and Wednesbury. This was extended to Bilston on 26 May 1923, by exercising running rights over the WDET tracks. The lease on the West Bromwich tracks ran out on 1 April 1924, and tram operations in that area were acquired by Birmingham Corporation. Darlaston depot then closed, not reopening until 1September 1928, following transfer of the remaining South Staffordshire routes, together with the Willenhall to Darlaston service, to Dudley, Stourbridge & District control, from August of that year.

Other moves in April included the transfer of the Dudley to Wednesbury route to the Dudley, Stourbridge and District Company, with the WDET taking control of the Darlaston to Wednesbury route and the joint services through Pleck to Walsall, which they continued to work with Walsall Corporation. This effectively brought to an end the operating days of the South Staffordshire Tramways.

Examples of services with frequencies and fares in 1914 are shown below

Route	Weekdays	Sundays	Fare
Dudley to Bilston (7 miles)	20 mins	AM 30 mins	5d (through)
	Sat PM 10 mins	PM 20 mins	
Bilston to Bradley (1.2 miles)	30 mins from 1.15pm	30 mins from 2.15pm	1d
	Sat eve 15mins		1½d return
Darlaston to Bilston (2 miles)	Day 30 mins	30 mins from 10.30am	1½d
	Eve 15 mins	15 mins from 1.30pm	
Bilston to Willenhall (1.6 miles)	30 mins	30 mins from 1.45pm	1½d
	Sat PM 10 mins	15 mins in evening	

A special service was also operated from Willenhall to Darlaston each day, with two workmen's cars at 5.30am. Otherwise, an evening weekday service was maintained on a 30-minute interval, including Sundays after 2.15pm, and a Saturday evening service operated on a 15-minute frequency. The fare was 1½d.

Fleet No	Into Service	Type	Builder	Truck	Seating
Steam Locos					
1-2	1883	4-wheel	Wilkinson		
3-12	1883	4-wheel	Beyer Peacock		
13-16	1883	4-wheel	Green		
17-21	1883	4-wheel	Wilkinson		
22-29	1884	4-wheel	Beyer Peacock		
30-37	1884	4-wheel	Green		
38	1885	4-wheel	Falcon		
Trailer Cars					
1-12	1883	D/Deck Canopy-top Bogie	Starbuck		Unknown
13-24	1883	D/Deck Canopy-top Bogie	Falcon		Unknown
25-34	1884	D/Deck Canopy-top Bogie	Falcon		Unknown
Electric Tramcars					
40-47	1892	D/Deck Open-top 4-wheel	Brown Marshall	Unknown	Unknown
48-55	1892	D/Deck Open-top 4-wheel	Lancaster Carriage & Wagon	Unknown	Unknown
1-4	1901	D/Deck Open-top 4-wheel	ERTCW	Brill 21E	22/22
5-9	1901	D/Deck Open-top 4-wheel	ERTCW	Brill 21E	22/22
10-27	1902	D/Deck Open-top Bogie	Brush	Brush	36/34
28-30	1903	D/Deck Open-top 4-wheel	Brush	Brush A	26/22
3	1911	D/Deck Top-covered 4-wheel	ERTCW	Brill 21E	26/22
31	1911	D/Deck Open-top 4-wheel	Brush	Brush L&C Radial	26/22
32-33	1911	D/Deck Top-covered 4-wheel	ERTCW	Brill 21E	26/22
34	1911	D/Deck Open-top 4-wheel	Brush	Brush L&C Radial	26/22
35	1911	D/Deck Top-covered 4-wheel	ERTCW	Brill 21E	26/22
36-37	1911	D/Deck Open-top 4-wheel	Brush	Brush L&C Radial	26/22
38	1911	D/Deck Top-covered 4-wheel	ERTCW	Brill 21E	26/22
39-51	1911	D/Deck Open-top 4-wheel	Brush	Brush L&C Radial	26/22
48	1911	D/Deck Open-top 4-wheel	ERTCW	Brush A	26/22
53-56	1911	D/Deck Open-top 4-wheel	ERTCW	Brush A	26/22
16	1911	D/Deck Open-top Bogie	City of Birmingham Tramways	Brush	34/28
57-60	1916	D/Deck	Brush	Brush	36/34

NOTES ON TRAMCARS

Nos 1-4 (1901 group). Had direct staircases, and in later life, canopy top-covers.

Nos 5-9. Had reversed staircases.

Nos 10-27. Had reversed staircases. Some cars later rebuilt as single deckers.

No 16 (1911 group). Had reversed staircases. Ex-City of Birmingham tramways No 179 and was supplied new to them in 1903.

Nos 28-30. Had reversed staircases.

Nos 3, 32-33, 35-38. Ex-Dudley, Stourbridge & District Electric Traction, from their 23-38 batch, and new to them in 1901.

Nos 31, 34, 36-37, 39-51. Exact origin uncertain but probably from either ex-Birmingham and Midland Tramways, from their 13-50 batch, and new to them in 1904, or ex-City of Birmingham Tramways, from their 192-256 batch, and new to them in 1904-5. All these cars had direct staircases and car 48 was later re-numbered 52.

Nos 48, 53-56. Ex-City of Birmingham Tramways, from their 151-171 batch, and new to them in 1901-2. These cars had direct staircases.

Nos 57-60. Ex-Wolverhampton District Electric Tramways, from their 14-30 batch, and new to them in 1902. These cars had reversed staircases.

N.B. – A number of cars were also received from the Birmingham & Midland Tramways, from their 1-12 batch, new to them in 1904; the total quantity and arrival dates are not known. They were double-deck, 4-wheel trams fitted with Bellamy tops, and built by Brush with AA type trucks. Upon receipt, they were allocated numbers of withdrawn or transferred cars.

Birmingham Area Lines

The history of Birmingham Corporation Tramways is a complex one, rightly deserving a separate publication, set as it was on the edge of the Black Country tramway network, and properly outside the remit of this book. The main area of common interest here lies in the Companies where the BET were actively involved, together with their lines and operations that were eventually absorbed into the Birmingham Corporation network.

In 1861, the Birmingham Improvement Act granted the Birmingham Corporation power to lay tramways for themselves. Over the years, many other local authorities also took an active part in the running of lines within their area. A prime example was West Bromwich Corporation who in 1902 purchased tramways within the borough, to lease out to the operating companies. In 1909 Dudley Corporation purchased the tramways in its borough, again leasing them back to the operating companies.

City of Birmingham Tramways Company Limited

This company had a somewhat turbulent history. It was formed as 'The British Electric Traction Company Limited' (BET) on 29 September 1896, with the intention of acquiring the Birmingham Central Tramways Company (BCTC) and converting the system to overhead electrification. It proved impossible to get the approval of Birmingham Corporation and after negotiations broke down on 7 June 1898, the company decided to proceed in any event with their intentions, overhead electric cars from the ERTCW works at Preston replacing the battery-electric ones on the Bristol Road route, on 14 May 1901.

Control of the BCTC eventually passed to the BET in June 1902. Following negotiations with neighbouring authorities, they promoted a Bill in 1903 to allow running powers over corporation tracks inside the city boundary. The incentive for this Bill stemmed from their alarm at the corporation's decision, reached on 7 March 1899, to work all tramways in the city themselves. Against a strong opposition, the Bill was defeated but through running by the company was allowed, thus avoiding the daunting prospect of all incoming cars terminating at the city boundary, with passengers having to change cars in both directions.

By 1903 Birmingham Corporation had obtained powers to operate tramways as the leases expired, and in 1904, the lease on the ex-Birmingham and Aston system duly ran out. As the corporation already owned all the tracks within the city, they took over this section of line and promptly electrified it, with UEC double-deck bogie cars working the re-opened line from Steelhouse Lane out to the boundary.

The City of Birmingham Tramway Company was granted a 21-year lease on the tracks of the former Birmingham and Aston Tramways Company effective from 9 June 1903; in June 1902, Aston Manor Urban District Council had purchased the section of line within its boundary, previously leased to the Birmingham and Aston Tramway Company. It was leased out to the City of Birmingham Tramway Company, with services commencing between Steelhouse Lane and Aston Church on 19 September 1904, Birmingham Corporation allowing through running over their electrified section. Unusually, the cars carried the coat of arms of Aston Manor UDC, although they were company property. Further routes were then opened: Six Ways to Victoria Road, on 27 October, and Gravelly Hill to Aston Cross, on 14 November, the later route being extended to Erdington on 22 April 1907.

The leases on the remaining City of Birmingham tracks continued to expire and were steadily taken over one by one by the corporation, with the majority ceasing on 31 December 1906 (also the last day of steam operation in Birmingham). On 30 June 1911 the lease on the routes to Selly Oak via Bristol Road and Cotteridge via Pershore Road finished, along with the cable tramway to Handsworth. The last operating right passed from the BET on 30 December 1911, along with 61 of the company's electric trams. Birmingham Corporation now had full control of all tracks within the city boundary, having absorbed several neighbouring smaller authorities in the process, and the way was clear for them to expand and unify the system.

Contact continued to be made by the corporation with the BET network at Handsworth, where it connected with the South Staffs tracks and at Ladywood with the Birmingham and Midland line. However, problems were now looming ever closer for the BET group, with the huge number of fixed life agreements made with local authorities, some of whom already had their own systems, which rubbed shoulders, not too comfortably, with the BET. The rot set in with a vengeance in 1924 when West Bromwich Corporation decided not to renew the relationship with the BET, the new lease on tracks inside their boundary passing in due course to Birmingham Corporation, mortally injuring the South Staffs operation and leaving a hole in the network. The BET structure became fragmented and non-viable, as the ex-South Staffs routes were transferred to the WDET and nearby DS&D operation. With the empire now dismembered, the end could not be fended off indefinitely, and by 1930 the B&MJTC had effectively gone and with it any hopes of an integrated Black Country network.

Birmingham District Power & Traction Company Limited

The origins of this company go back to the Birmingham and Western Districts Tramway Order of 1881. A line from Summer Row to the city boundary was constructed by Birmingham Corporation, the service commencing on 6 July 1885, using Kitson steam tram locos and Oldbury trailer cars. It was leased to and worked by the Birmingham & Midland Tramways Limited, newly formed on 22 November 1883. The service to Dudley commenced on 30 August 1885, but the operation was not a financial success, with the branch to West Bromwich closing 1892-1893.

The company was sold in 1899, and in February 1900 came under the control of the BET, who obtained the necessary local authority leases to electrify the system, the branches along Bromford Lane and Spon Lane into West Bromwich being the first to open on 3 November 1903. Cars from the South Staffordshire Tramways temporarily worked them, as the new electric cars had not yet been delivered to the Birmingham and Midland. The main Dudley route opened to electric cars on 19 November 1904, together with a new line from Cape Hill into Bearwood. Finally, on 31 December the line along Heath Street to the city boundary was brought into service. Constructed by the Birmingham and Western Districts Tramway Company in 1886 it had lain unused. This section was extended to Soho Station in Smethwick on 25 May 1905.

As part of their expansionist plans for a Black Country network, the BET formed the Birmingham and Midland Joint Tramways Committee on 4 December 1903. This encompassed a number of operators including Dudley, Stourbridge & District, Kinver Light Railway, South Staffordshire, Wolverhampton District and Birmingham & Midland. Much rationalisation was achieved with through running and timetabling across the system, plus a common fare structure. By 1907, Tividale Works, just to the east of Dudley, was producing and maintaining tramcars for the burgeoning empire.

The lease on lines within the city expired on 30 June 1906. From this point, all short workings in the city were covered by Birmingham Corporation, with the company continuing to work the through service to Dudley and West Bromwich. The company name changed on 13 August 1912 to the Birmingham District Power and Traction Company Limited. On 1 April 1928, Birmingham Corporation assumed control of the main line to Dudley, the West Bromwich branches transferring to the BET group's Dudley, Stourbridge & District Electric Traction Company. From this point on, the Birmingham District Power and Traction Company ceased to be a tramway operator.

High St Wollaston

High St Wollaston

Dudley, Stourbridge & District Electric Traction Company tram 57 at the Fish Inn in June 1929.

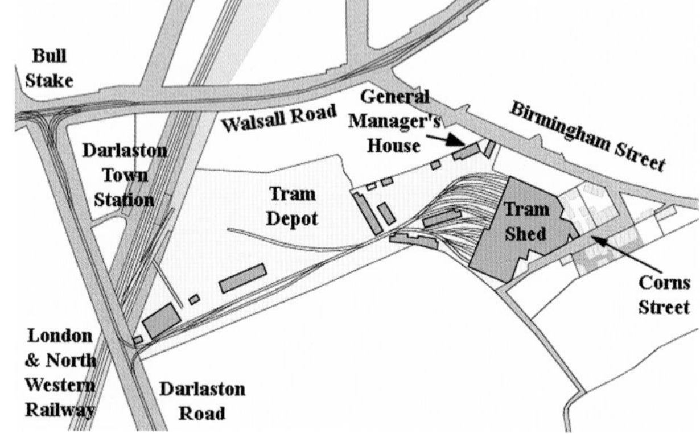

Darlaston tram depot

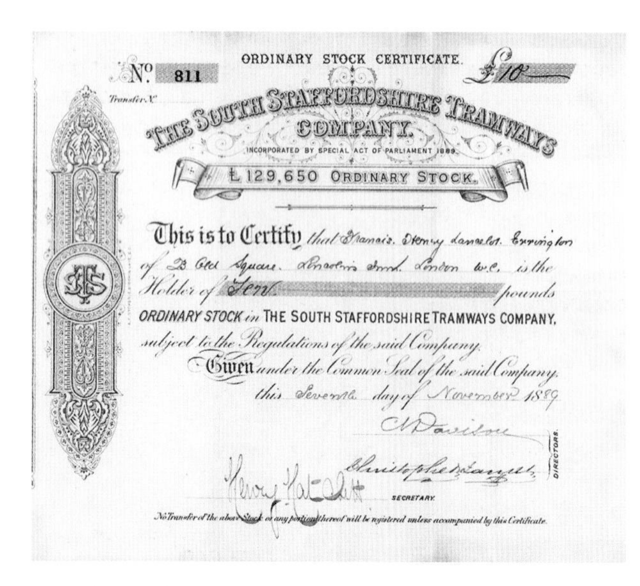

No. 811 ORDINARY STOCK CERTIFICATE. £10

Transfer No.

THE SOUTH STAFFORDSHIRE TRAMWAYS COMPANY.

INCORPORATED BY SPECIAL ACT OF PARLIAMENT 1889.

£129,650 ORDINARY STOCK.

This is to Certify that Francis Henry Lancelot Errington of 23 Old Square Lincoln's Inn London W.C. is the Holder of Ten pounds ORDINARY STOCK in THE SOUTH STAFFORDSHIRE TRAMWAYS COMPANY, subject to the Regulations of the said Company.

Given under the Common Seal of the said Company, this Seventh day of November 1889

[illegible] [illegible] DIRECTORS.

[illegible] SECRETARY.

No Transfer of the above Stock or any portion thereof will be registered unless accompanied by this Certificate.

South Staffordshire Tramways ordinary stock certificate.

South Staffordshire steam tram and crew at Dudley

Author's collection

CHAPTER 5 The Lorain System from its Inception in 1902

The decision was taken to use the new orporation power supply in the event of electrification. The Municipal Lighting Works had been built in 1894 on a site adjacent to Commercial Road, the Mayor, Alderman Charles T Mander, laying the foundation stone on Monday 21 May in the presence of other Councillors and the Rector, Prebendary Jeffcock, amidst much pomp and ceremony, with the Mayor afterwards providing suitable entertainment for the dignitaries at the Victoria Hotel. Although originally intended for lighting the town and surrounding area, (capable of generating sufficient electricity to light 10,000 lamps with upgrading to 15,000) the equipment was quite suitable for providing power to the tramway system. Tram services now running were –

Queen Square to Newbridge, every fifteen minutes
Queen Square to Ettingshall Road, every twenty minutes
Snow Hill to Dudley, every forty minutes

Around this time, a decision was made to convert to 3ft 6in gauge tracks, which were already used by the BET group across the Black Country. Electrification was then considered and discussed in depth. The local daily newspaper, the Express & Star, campaigned unsuccessfully for a traditional system of overhead supply. The council had formed a Tramways Committee in 1896 and debates were held in that year, and in 1899 and 1900, to discuss the matter of electrification. Chairman of the Tramways Committee was Alderman Mander. He had been elected as Chairman at the first meeting on 9 October 1896, holding down the position of Mayor at the same time. A number of influential Wulfrunians, led by Alderman Mander, were quite strongly opposed to the erection of wiring and traction poles on both environmental and visual grounds, being more in favour of the largely unknown Lorain system of stud contact, Alderman Mander stating that he would never allow wiring to disfigure the streets of Wolverhampton.

His attention had been drawn to an invention of William Milton Brown of Johnstown, Pennsylvania, USA. This quite unique method of surface contact current collection, known as the Brown Underground System, had been briefly trialled by him in 1898 on the Washington and Congress Heights Railway in Washington D.C. In 1895, his patent for the stud had been assigned to the Johnston Steel Company of Lorain, Ohio.

This company had its origins in the form of one James Arthur Moxham (1854-1931), a Welsh-born steel manufacturer. Originally from Neath, Glamorganshire, Moxham moved to Louisville, Kentucky, in 1869 and found employment in an iron foundry until 1878. Later, in Alabama, he was to be found putting the Birmingham Rolling Mill in order, an occupation he was to successfully maintain until 1883, when he moved again, to a relatively new town called Johnstown, in Pennsylvania, to set up and direct the construction of iron girder rails.

Johnstown was a growing community, founded in 1793 by Swiss immigrant Joseph Johns, and started to prosper with the building of the Pennsylvania Railroad and the Cambria Iron Works; by 1889, it had a population of some 30,000 people and a growing reputation for the quality of its steel products. Moxham was to rise to prominence and no little fame that year, by helping to direct the rebuilding of Johnstown, following the flood disaster. Johnstown had been built in a river valley on the Appalachian Plateau, and on June 1 of that year at 4.07 pm, 14 miles up the Little Conemaugh River, the old and poorly maintained south fork dam broke. This privately-owned structure, which held back the waters of the three-mile-long Lake Conemaugh, collapsed, flooding the town some 450 feet below with 20 million tons of water and a huge amount of debris, taking all before it and tragically claiming the lives of 2209 people.

Mimicking the life pattern of its owner, the Johnson Steel Company then moved to Ohio, with the site being completed and operational by 1895, subsequently refinancing as the Lorain Steel Company. In 1898, the concern was sold to the Federal Steel Company, who also owned the Illinois Steel Company at Chicago, the Lorain Steel Company merging with Illinois Steel in 1899, and the whole enterprise becoming part of U S Steel in 1901.

The Lorain system of stud contact used metal studs 12¾in x 6¾in, connected underground to the electricity supply, and these were sunk into the road between the tram rails, at about nine to ten feet intervals, but closer on curves and hills. The studs had a cast iron head, inside which was a renewable non-magnetic manganese steel centre insert. Inside this was a movable strip of soft iron forming an armature, and connected to the power supply by a 1½in-wide 'Z-shaped' copper strip spring holding the armature away from the stud head. Carbon contacts were fitted to both the armature top and the underside of the stud head, the whole mechanism being contained in an insulated cup, in turn surrounded by insulating oil. The whole unit was bolted to a reconstructed granite block, which sat ¾in above the surrounding road surface. The main power supply cable was laid underground between the tracks in a wooden trough filled with bitumen, and the studs were connected to the power line by brass plugs and sockets, allowing for easy maintenance and removal.

Fastened underneath the tram was a centrally located 12ft-long phosphor-bronze metal skate, insulated from the tram body by a flexible rubber tube and in turn fastened to a wooden support. The rubber tube depressed the skate into contact with the studs. Either side of this were two 16ft-long skates, fixed 2in above the road and magnetised by six pairs of strong electromagnets connected by iron strips and energised by the traction power supply. These ensured that a stud was always live before the 12ft pickup skate reached it; there was also a facility for rechargeable battery back-up to energise the first stud after power disconnection.

In operation, as the magnetic skate passed over the stud, the armature was drawn upwards to the stud head, completing the electrical circuit. The 12ft skate then made contact with the stud, drawing current for the motor. As the 16ft skate cleared the stud, with the magnetic field no longer there, the armature dropped down and broke the circuit, the stud ceasing to be live. The additional length of the magnetic skate ensured that there was no arcing after each stud had been used and that a stud would always be live in advance of the tramcar using it. Lightweight earthing chains hanging from the end of the tram completed the arrangements and would, in theory, make contact with any rogue stud remaining live and short circuit it.

All tramcars carried batteries for use in energising magnets if the line current was switched off. Once over a live stud, the magnets would continue to be powered from it. The battery was also useful in the event of stranding on a dead stud. As insufficient power was generated in normal service, batteries were usually taken off and charged up overnight. Over the years, there have been many tales told of horses being electrocuted by rogue studs remaining live, but without foundation. It is a sad fact that horses were treated badly and generally overworked, with these tales probably stemming from an incident in Pipers Row on 24 May 1902, when a horse dropped dead in the street, a not uncommon occurrence. It is however known that the corporation did on one occasion pay compensation to the Great Western Railway.

Track laying at the junction of the Tettenhall Road with Newhampton Road, in 1901/2. This is now the main A41 road to Shrewsbury and Newport. Cliff Brown collection courtesy John Hughes

The same scene as viewed from Newhampton Road. This was the only triangular junction on the system and as such was used not just for emergency working, but to turn trams around, thereby evening out the wear on the wheel sets.

Looking through Queen Square from the top of Darlington Street, as construction of the new 3ft 6in gauge track takes place. The tracks to the right in the foreground will go down Victoria Street, whilst the right-hand tracks above were intended for cars terminating in Queen Square; the 'main line' running on along Lichfield Street as far as Victoria Square and the drive leading to the railway station.

Images Cliff Brown collection courtesy John Hughes

Following the decision to convert to electric operation, the Tramways Committee initially opted for an overhead system and in November 1900 invited tenders for the supply of equipment. March 1901 saw the committee in receipt of several tenders, but dithering by committee members saw further special meetings in April, due to continuing pressure from Alderman Mander and his supporters, at which the merits of a surface contact system were again argued. After some deliberation, the committee decided to recommend the adoption of the Lorain Surface Contact System and agreement was reached on 6 May with the Lorain company's London office to equip a one-mile experimental section of track and assess its suitability for use in Wolverhampton.

All other preparations and contracts for the erection of overhead equipment were immediately stopped, though work on the track was allowed to continue, as were orders for tramcars. A section of track from Cleveland Road to Ettingshall Road, especially constructed in 1901 for the Corporation Tramways Department was suitably altered. The track had been put in at the time as a newly-erected and purpose-built depot in Cleveland Road. Built in brick and stone, it bore the carved legend 'MUNICIPAL TRAMWAYS CAR DEPOT', on the building frontage. The administrative offices were transferred to Cleveland Road from Darlington Street during 1902 and

A section of the rail used by the electric trams.

This is the main tramways switchboard, shown about 1903. Commercial Road Power Station was opened in 1894 and was to supply power for the entire Corporation Tramways (and subsequently trolleybus) operation. Its original function was to supply electric power to the residents and businesses in the town. Cliff Brown collection courtesy John Hughes

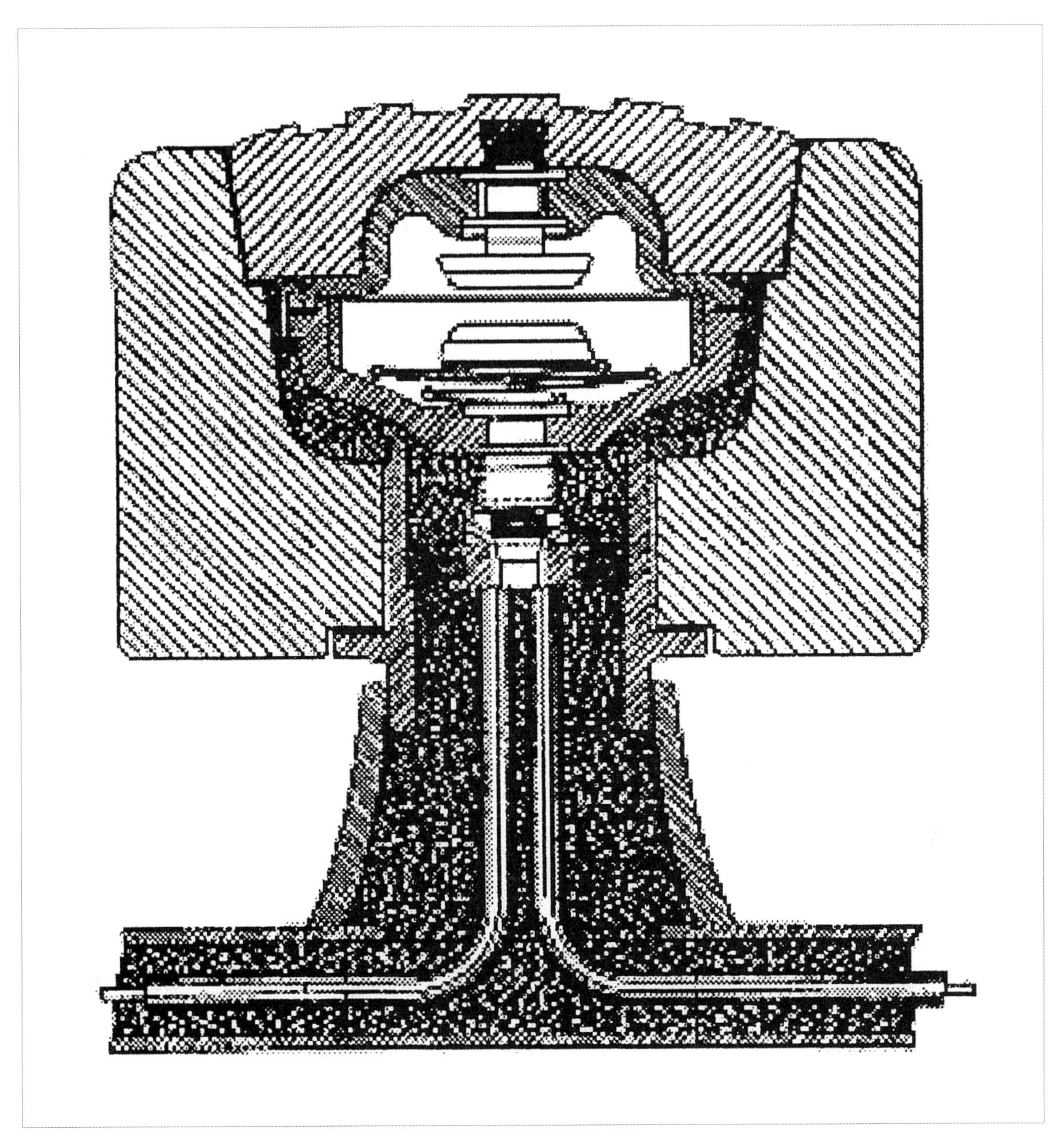

Detailed drawing of a Lorain stud. Author's collection

the depot subsequently added to in 1904, 1909, 1913 and 1921, eventually covering the site of the town's original open-air cattle market as far as Transport Road. A final expansion took place in 1932, taking in the last available plot in Cleveland Road.

The experimental section of track was ready by 14 January 1902, but did not open until 6 February and being extended in due course to Stow Heath Lane on 24 September to meet the BET overhead line from Bilston. The service was every ten minutes and after a successful thirty days trial, the corporation then agreed to conversion of the remaining ten and a half miles of line at a cost of £3 700 per mile, initially on a twelve-month trial basis, though full acceptance was achieved in due course. Wolverhampton Corporation was to be the only UK operator of the Lorain system, and one of only two worldwide if the brief foray on the Washington and Congress Heights Railway is included!

Wolverhampton Corporation could not, of course, purchase lines into Bilston, Sedgley, Willenhall or Darlaston without BET consent, this being subsequently obtained on agreement that all routes would eventually be electrified, though the method was not qualified at the time.

A selection of parts to make up an operational Lorain stud. Author's collection

Newbridge in 1901. Laying track and looking towards Wolverhampton. Author's collection

Newhampton Road, looking towards Whitmore Reans from the Newbridge end. Author's collection

Looking down Waterloo Road towards Bushbury, (Wolverhampton Wanderers' football ground is currently just to the right). The centre duct for the Lorain system can clearly be seen. Author's collection

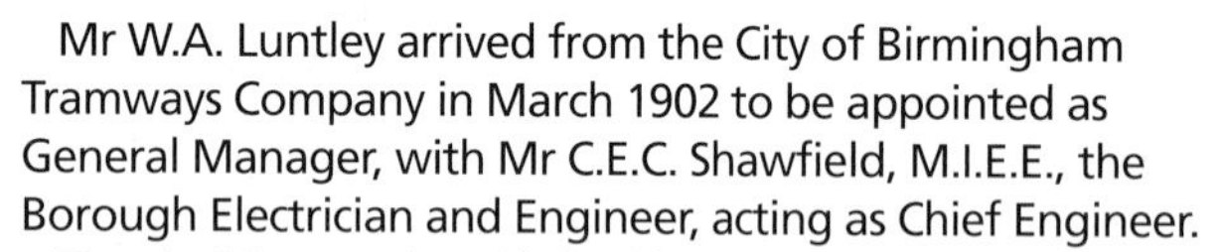

Mr W.A. Luntley arrived from the City of Birmingham Tramways Company in March 1902 to be appointed as General Manager, with Mr C.E.C. Shawfield, M.I.E.E., the Borough Electrician and Engineer, acting as Chief Engineer.

The decision to electrify had been lent impetus by the impending Wolverhampton Industrial and Arts Exhibition, to be opened in the West Park by the Duke and Duchess of Connaught on 1 May 1902 and run throughout the summer. As a prestige event, it was felt essential for the town that a modern style of transport should be available to carry Wulfrunians and visitors alike to the venue. The contractor laboured night and day to have the new service ready, with the line opening just in time on the morning of 1 May as the exhibition opened. It provided an excellent transport link from the railway station, essential in the days before mass ownership of the private car.

During May, a contract was issued to equip the whole of the street tramway system and any future extension. Until the trials concluded, the installation remained the property of the Lorain Company, who had the power to remove equipment should it prove to be unsuccessful. William Milton Brown continued to work for the steel company throughout the manufacture of the studs and would be based at Cleveland Road during 1903 to oversee installation. Dudley Street and Queen Street were not electrified, and consequently fell into disuse, as Lichfield Street had now become the main thoroughfare from Queen Square to Victoria Square and the London & North Western Railway Company station. Work had already started on narrowing the track gauge to 3ft 6in, with the first three routes being opened soon after Lady Day on 25 March. The Corporation also placed orders for the first twelve electric trams to be supplied, from two different manufacturers, with four varieties of motor and electrical equipment from the main suppliers, for comparison purposes, as follows -

Three Electric Railway & Tramway Carriage Works (ERTCW)/Dick, Kerr motor
Three Milnes/British Thompson Houston (BTH) motor
Three Milnes/Westinghouse motor
Three Milnes/Lorain motor

Only the Lorain-motored cars had arrived in time for the opening in February. They had non-vestibule bodies

A view of Cleveland Road depot in late 1902. As the fleet grows, the available space is rapidly being taken up; cars 17 and 19 arrived in August of that year.

Below: Outside the depot with cars 1 and 32. Note the WERGS ROAD destination on car 32, which would be working the Tettenhall Road service. The picture has been taken at the east end of the depot and alongside the Newmarket public house, which was to survive until the end of trolleybus operation.

Images Cliff Brown collection courtesy John Hughes

supplied by George F Milnes from his Hadley Castle Works in Shropshire, opened in 1900. The three trams were on Lorain-Du Pont trucks, and fitted with life guards. They were numbered 10-12, being respectively a single deck combination car ('toast rack'/saloon/'toast rack') seating 8+16+8, an open-top double-decker with reversed staircase with seating for 26 on top and 22 below and a closed single-deck saloon seating 26 (the only other place in the UK where Du Pont trucks were seen was Dublin, where they were used extensively).

The remaining cars entered service in May. A new livery of olive green with gamboge upper decks and end sheets was introduced. Lining was in gold with elaborate corners and the Borough Coat of Arms on waist panels. Following the experimental success, sections were then opened as follows –

Cleveland Road to Victoria Square – 30 April 1902
Victoria Square to Coleman Street – 1 May 1902
Victoria Square to Newbridge (via Chapel Ash)
– 12 June 1902
Coleman Street to Newbridge – 11 August 1902
Newbridge to Wergs Road (Dog and Gun)
– 13 September 1902
Waterloo Road to Molineux (football ground siding)
– 20 September 1902

Newly-delivered Combination Car No 10 outside Cleveland Road depot in 1902.

A picture of car 11 outside Cleveland Road depot in 1902, complete with 'extras'.

Cars 12 and 11.

Images Cliff Brown collection courtesy John Hughes

Car 12 outside Cleveland Road depot, with the old cattle market in the background, from which land would eventually be taken for the depot extension programme.

Car 12, manned by Corporation officials for photographic purposes. The 'Providence' lifeguard was soon changed to a more compact pattern, using the 'Wilson Bennet' metal grid type.

Images Cliff Brown collection courtesy John Hughes

Lorain tram 11 in Cleveland Road, the event being either inspection day on 14 January 1902 or opening day on 6 February 1902. Forders Royal Hansom Carriage Manufactory made some early motor bus bodies.

Stubbs Lane terminus of the Penn Fields route on opening day, 10 September 1909. Several local dignitaries travelled on the special car.

Images Cliff Brown collection courtesy John Hughes

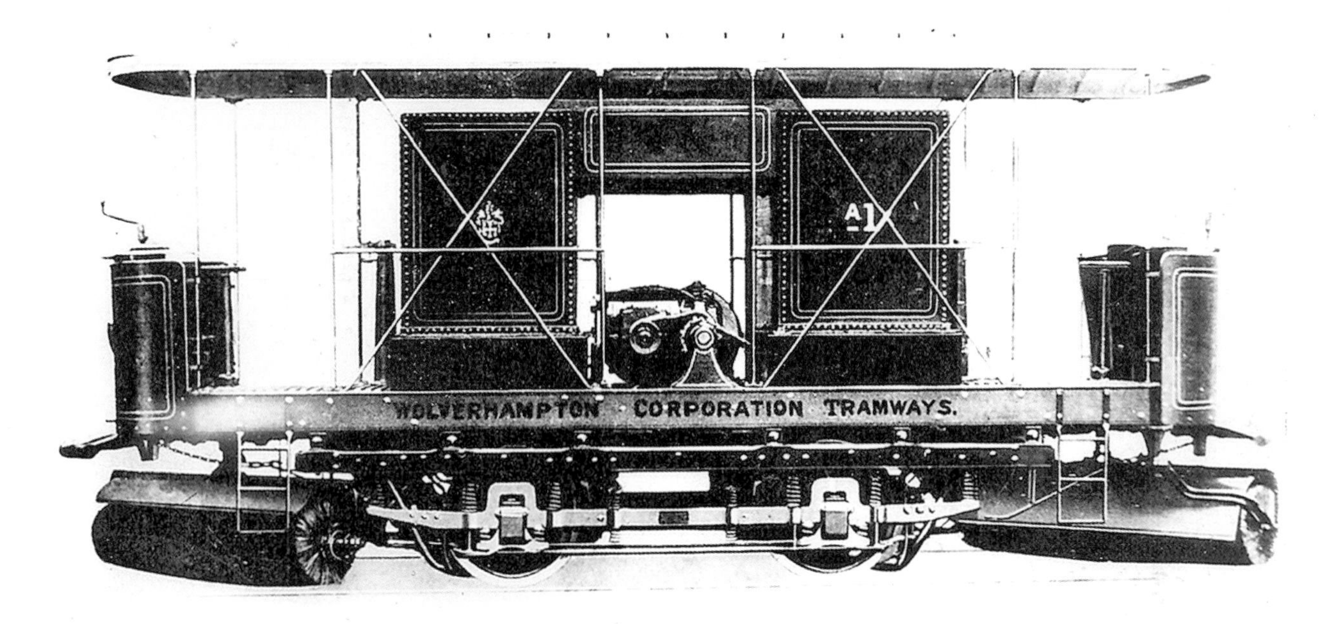

Works car A1, the combined Snow Plough, Track Sweeper and Waterer, built by Dick, Kerr in 1902/3 and fitted with a Brill 21E modified truck. Cliff Brown collection courtesy John Hughes

By July 1902, the Providence American-type lifeguards on cars 10-12 had been replaced by Wilson Bennett metal grid type. On 17 April 1903, just prior to the end of the 12-month trial period of the Lorain system, the Borough Electrical Engineer made a proposal, suggesting that the council consider motorbus operation as an alternative to further tramway construction, and in August of that year a Milnes Daimler vehicle was provided, Milnes supplying its own driver. It operated for five days on the Dudley route, but the idea was not pursued. Changes were also made to the transverse 'toast rack' seats in the open ends of combination cars 2/4/7 and 10; these were altered to longitudinal, increasing the seating from eight to nine (but often carrying 10) excluding the driver. Side destination signs were also introduced across the fleet.

Meanwhile, on 20 May the councillors met for the third time to consider acceptance and purchase of the Lorain system. After considerable debate and much correspondence with the Lorain company, agreement to purchase was reached on 21 September.

The decision was not made without much soul searching and was driven in part by the fixation to keep BET out of Wolverhampton, the flames, and fears, still being fanned by the Tramways Committee Chairman, Alderman Mander in his personal and misguided crusade against the company. This was followed on 12 October by approval for the construction of further extensions to the surface contact system and reconstruction of some existing sections. Lines then opened in 1904 were –

Snow Hill to Fighting Cocks	8 March	Dudley Road
Horseley Fields to Coventry Street	2 April	Willenhall Road
Coventry Street to Deans Road	23 April	Willenhall Road
Princes Square to Church Street	22 June	Wednesfield Road
Waterloo Road to Bushbury Lane	12 August	Stafford Road
Church Street to New Street	31 October	Wednesfield Road

The opening to New Street completed the second stage of electrification. In later years, the Whitmore Reans route was extended to a new terminus at Hunter Street on 26 January 1905, with one timetabled workmens' through car each day to Tettenhall via the three-way junction at Newbridge. As for the fate of the two horse tram depots, the one at the bottom of Darlington Street was let to the Water Department in 1904 and eventually sold on, with Newbridge being sold in part to a Mr A Wilkes in 1911 and the rest going to the Wolverhampton Corporation Electricity Department.

The Wolverhampton Corporation Tramways Act 1904 allowed for future extensions to the tramway system, including provision for motorbus operation in connection with them. These powers were used in 1905 during the construction of the Penn Fields route, with Wolseley double deck motorbuses operating a service

Above: An interior view of Cleveland Road tram depot shortly after opening. The building still has that new-look to it. Note the fashionable globe light fittings. Cliff Brown collection courtesy John Hughes

Below: A view of Cleveland Road depot in 1902. The stone wording above the middle door was to survive intact until the end of trolleybus operation. Cliff Brown collection courtesy John Hughes

Car 8 and crew are seen at Cleveland Road depot during the period 1914 – 1918. Author's collection

between School Street and Stubbs Lane, until 20 July 1909, when it was suspended to allow for completion of track laying, with the tram route opening on 10 September 1909.

Four motorbuses in total were used, being of 20hp and using flat horizontally-opposed engines with a chain final drive. Seating was for 18 outside, 16 inside and two beside the driver, with a rear outside staircase. The first vehicle was registration number O-WY-39, on loan from 1 September 1905 until 2 October that year and eventually sold for further service in Russia. The remaining buses were registration numbers DA 108, DA 109 and DA 110. They were licensed on 24 October 1905 and withdrawn in 1909. DA 108 was sold in 1910 to Henry Querney of 56 Victoria Street, Birmingham and modified to run as a low-sided lorry; it was scrapped on 6 September 1920. DA 110 was sold on in 1909 to T Lander of Bromsgrove, to be used as a single deck vehicle, being finally de-licensed on 20 November 1912. This action effectively made Wolverhampton the first municipal tramway undertaking to operate motorbuses.

Laying down of the surface contact system also necessitated the widening of Worcester Street and reconstruction of Queen Square, with its attendant track. Notwithstanding the fact that operating costs for overhead electric wires were now only about half that of surface contact tracks, the Corporation continued to plough their own politically motivated furrow with the Lorain system, thus keeping BET at bay. The increased costs from a mixed system precluded it from being considered, in the eyes of a cost-conscious corporation. During 1905, Mr H. Vickers AMIEE succeeded Mr Shawfield as engineer.

Since superseding horse traction with electrically powered trams, through services to Dudley, Bilston and Willenhall had ceased due to differing methods of current collection – the BET area surrounding Wolverhampton using overhead collection exclusively, which effectively isolated the corporation with their continued use of the surface collection Lorain system, to the rejection of all other forms of current supply. Representations from the public, unhappy with the inconvenience of disjointed operation, persuaded the corporation to make a further approach to the BET in February 1905, to reconsider the possibility of through working. On these routes, passengers would walk between the joint termini at the boundary to make a through journey. As a result of the discussions, a number of double-deck corporation cars were fitted with nearside trolley poles for overhead working, whilst several BET cars underwent fitting of surface contact skates and the attendant equipment.

The corporation and WDET resumed joint services with dual-equipped cars, from Victoria Square through to Bilston Town Hall on 9 November 1905, and to Willenhall market place on 18 April 1906. A number of corporation double-deck cars were equipped with side-fitted overhead trolley booms for working on the company owned section of the Bilston route, these being 19-24 and 25-28. On the company section of the Willenhall route, the corporation fitted out single-deck Lorain cars

Left: An excellent picture of the underside of car 12 in Cleveland Road depot. This view, taken from the maintenance pit, shows the collection equipment and skates to advantage.

Cliff Brown collection courtesy John Hughes

1, 5, 7, 10 and at least one other, 39, with overhead equipment for current collection. BET dual-equipped cars did not start through running on the Dudley route for 12 months, until 15 October 1906.

In deference to the joint nature of operation, tickets issued on these services bore the names of both operators. From 15 October, ten suitably equipped BET four-wheel cars were also able to work into Snow Hill from Dudley; a short section of track was laid across the junction at Parkfield Road to physically connect the termini of the two systems. A further extension on 1 May 1907 allowed company cars to work through from Fighting Cocks to Darlaston. The corporation now operated through to Bilston and Willenhall using their tramcars only, while the BET Wolverhampton District cars had the monopoly on the route to Dudley. The through service proved to be of limited success as the BET cars ran much slower due in some part to the extra ton of weight gained when the surface contact equipment was added.

Princes Square in 1902; the newly-completed Royal London Building dominates the scene, with car 3 approaching. The Wednesfield route, which will lead off to the right, has not yet been connected.

Lichfield Street, viewed from Princes Square. Another tram can just be seen, parked on one of the Victoria Square stubs used by services entering from Ettingshall Road.

In this busy scene, the photographer is looking down Lichfield Street, past the Art Gallery on the left, and with Queen Square behind him

Queen Square, as seen from the balcony of the Queens Cinema around 1921; the presence of traction poles indicates the impending change to the overhead system.

A view of Darlington Street in the early 1900s, seen from the junction with Waterloo Road. Car 16 is approaching with a service from Tettenhall. To the right are the Gas Company's offices and across the way lies the Methodist Church. With its spire rising dimly in the distance at the foot of Darlington Street, is St Mark's Church in Chapel Ash.

On a snowy winter's day, a tram passes St Mark's Church in Chapel Ash and prepares to climb Darlington Street to Queen Square.

Images Cliff Brown collection courtesy John Hughes

An inward-bound tram is seen near St Jude's Church. From the postmark showing through, the illustration appears to be from a popular postcard of the time. Author's collection

A period scene on the Tettenhall Road by Newbridge, as a tram heads towards St Jude's Church and back to Wolverhampton. Cliff Brown collection courtesy John Hughes

Car 17 is seen at Tettenhall terminus. Note the very rural surroundings and the abrupt termination of both the tracks and cobbled stone setts. The town of Wolverhampton was then very much smaller than it is now, and open countryside was quickly reached. Cliff Brown collection courtesy John Hughes

A tram waits at the Coleman Street terminus around 1903/5. This stub eventually fell out of use; the trams proceeding from right to left across the view, as they continued down Newhampton Road to a terminus at Hunter Street. Cliff Brown collection courtesy John Hughes

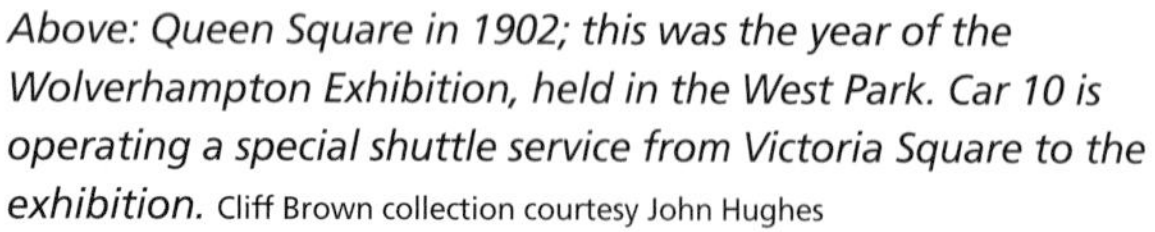

Above: Queen Square in 1902; this was the year of the Wolverhampton Exhibition, held in the West Park. Car 10 is operating a special shuttle service from Victoria Square to the exhibition. Cliff Brown collection courtesy John Hughes

Above, right: Newly laid tracks at the bottom of Newhampton Road. Despite the effort involved in laying this section, it never saw regular timetabled services, being used for occasional workings and kept as an alternative emergency route to Newbridge and Tettenhall. Cliff Brown collection courtesy John Hughes

Right: A car is seen passing through Queen Square on its way to the Industrial and Arts Exhibition, held in the West Park in 1902, and it will use the Whitmore Reans track for this purpose. Author's collection

An early view of Bushbury terminus, at the junction of Bushbury Lane and Stafford Road. Such was the expansion of the town in later years that this point was probably less than half way to the eventual terminus of the replacement trolleybus service, at Fordhouses. Cliff Brown collection courtesy John Hughes

This view of Queen Square was taken in 1913 and shows the horse bus service waiting to depart for Compton, on the road to Bridgnorth in Shropshire. Of the three trams that are (just) visible, the centre (top-covered) tram is on route to Penn Fields.
Cliff Brown collection courtesy John Hughes

Car 44 is seen in Lichfield Street as it sets off past the Grand Theatre for Penn Fields. The tracks coming from the left of the picture give access to Cleveland Road depot via Victoria Square.
Author's collection

The year is 1909. Car 30 is about to descend Victoria Street. The Queens Arcade (shown behind the tram) has recently been completed; Wolverhampton's first covered shopping centre! The second tram is heading for Tettenhall; the destination boards reading 'WERGS' – the district immediately beyond the terminus was, and still is, on the Wergs Road.

In 1910, with the Empire Palace Variety Theatre in the background, UEC car 44 reaches the top of Victoria Street and turns into Queen Square. The modern-day House of Fraser (ex Beattie's) shop occupies the area immediately to the left of the picture.

A tram in the passing loop in Worcester Street approaches Great Brickkiln Street as it heads for Penn Fields.

Cars pass on the Penn Fields route at the junction of Lea Road and Penn Road. St Peter's Church can be seen distantly in the background. The tram car going to town is waiting at the loop exit, as a car bound for Penn Fields enters the long serpentine passing loop, which is laid out in a large sweeping curve into Lea Road.

Images Cliff Brown collection courtesy John Hughes

Penn Road in 1902, with the tram tracks peeling off into the start of Lea Road. The Lorain studs are clearly evident in the stone setts between the rails.

Stubbs Lane, as viewed from Lea Road, in 1909. The terminus is just a few hundred yards beyond the tram, at the junction with the main Penn Road.

Stubbs Lane terminus, for the Penn Fields route, with Penn Fields district lying a quarter of a mile behind the tram. The road running across the picture is the Penn Road, with semi-open countryside to the left and Wolverhampton some two miles to the right.

Images Cliff Brown collection courtesy John Hughes

During 1907/8 the cars fitted with the Wilson Bennett metal grid type of lifeguard were refitted with the later Hudson & Bowring lath type. Early in 1909, the BET advised Wolverhampton Corporation that they could not carry on supporting the through working services, and would only continue to do so if the corporation would now convert the section to the overhead system. BET had failed to show any increase in their revenue and usage of electricity had increased with the fitting of the heavier Lorain equipment. Lack of properly-trained staff and maintenance facilities had also contributed to the situation. The corporation declined the request as unacceptable and all through working terminated with effect from 10 January 1909, WDET cars on the Dudley route reverting to Dudley – Fighting Cocks – Darlaston working. Through running was only to resume on 26 March 1921 when Wolverhampton finally converted to overhead wiring supply. Corporation services to Bilston and Willenhall reverted to the borough boundary in the meanwhile.

Services to Wednesfield and Willenhall continued to be operated by single-deck trams due to low-height railway

Bilston Road, at Stowheath Lane junction, effectively the end of the Corporation's Lorain-style tramway lines. At this point, through passengers would have to change to a car of the WDET system; one indeed can be seen waiting in the distance at the limit of the overhead wiring. Cliff Brown collection courtesy John Hughes

A tramcar in Lichfield Street passes over the emergency cross-over in Princess Square; the destination is shown as Bilston Road. This poses a bit of a mystery as the car is coming from the direction of Queen Square and cross-town working was not generally in use at this time. Author's collection

bridges on Broad Street and at Horseley Fields. On 10 September 1909, the motorbus service to Penn Fields was converted to operation by tram, the Wolseley motorbuses being disposed of. Running to Stubbs Lane via Lea Road, this was to be the last tram route to be opened, with operation now at its greatest extent, giving a system of some 21½ miles of single track across a little over 13¾ route miles, the whole now being supported by a fleet of 45 double-deck and seven single-deck tramcars. With the exception of the Snow Hill to Dudley line, all services initially operated out of Victoria Square. Trailing crossovers were subsequently laid, allowing the Wednesfield terminal to be moved out to Princes Square, the service from Willenhall now operating to the top of Five Ways. During business hours, there was a further extension of the Whitmore Reans service to Riches Street, which was charged at an additional half penny. This proved to be unpopular, and was of short duration.

The year 1910/11 saw an extremely bad winter, during which many crews went down with pneumonia. This speeded up the fitting of vestibules to a number of cars and also top covers, some council members opposing this action on the grounds that it could well result in top-heavy trams! Elongated wooden-framed destination indicators were also fitted, initially using separately supplied name panels that located in guide slots, and finally converting to more modern illuminated roller panels. By 1912, the undertaking was in a favourable position financially, and started to contribute each year to the relief of rates programme.

The first private motor bus service in the borough commenced on 13 March 1911, when a Mr C L Wells introduced a working from Wolverhampton's London & North Western Railway station to Kingswinford; the corporation were quick to impose a protective minimum fare within the boundary. On 7 September the corporation commenced operating their own 30-minute service between Queen Square and Thorneycroft Lane, using a 24-seat Albion bus. There had been some industrial development in the Park Lane area and this was seen as a cheaper option to a tramway extension. In 1914, two more half hourly services were introduced; to Compton and the Rose & Crown at Penn, both operating from Victoria Square. Four Albion single-deck buses were provided, but the services had to be suspended when the War Office requisitioned the chassis. The route to the Rose & Crown was eventually destined to undergo a metamorphosis as a trolleybus service.

During 1913-1914 the Great Western Railway Company commenced construction of a branch line to Wombourne village. The line was to pass through Newbridge parallel to the existing canal system. For a period of time, the main road was severed and the triangle of points at the junction with New Hampton Road West brought back into daily use as a terminus point. A solitary tram was left at Tettenhall the night before the road was lifted, and worked a shuttle service between there and the bottom of the 'Rock' to connect with tramcars from town until completion of all road work.

In this view, a tram has arrived from Fighting Cocks and is dropping down Snow Hill to the terminus. Cliff Brown collection courtesy John Hughes

Car 30 pictured at Fighting Cocks in the early 1900s. The building behind the tram is almost certainly the Fighting Cocks Inn. Author's collection

The tramcar depot at Cleveland Road was also extended westward around this time. This was essential, as further purchases had increased the fleet to 52 trams plus two snowploughs and a salt car. Numbers 19-24 were unique in never having their reversed staircases changed to normal position. Route numbers were introduced around 1915, initially displayed on the car headlamps. They were

1 – Tettenhall
2 – Whitmore Reans
3 – Bushbury
4 – Penn Fields
5 – Willenhall
6 – Wednesfield
7 – Bilston
8 – Fighting Cocks

In the early 1920s they were moved to the roof area, using purpose-built service number boxes. Indicators on the tram sides displayed both route terminals. Railway Station was shown for Victoria Square-bound trams, though they terminated some two hundred yards short of the railway itself.

CHAPTER 6 | The War Years 1914-1918

On 4 August 1914, Britain was plunged into conflict and the advent of World War 1 (1914-1918), as it became known, resulted in the need for many economies across the country as a whole, in particular the consumption of electricity, as production of coal fell. Measures taken by the Corporation Tramways Department included the termination of inward bound services on routes 1, 2 and 3 at Queen Square, made possible by use of an existing reversing stub, leaving one car to work a shuttle service between there and Victoria Square. Route 4 now only came as far as the top of Victoria Street. All of this was designed to reduce current consumption, though it proved to be unpopular with the travelling public, due to the inevitable inconvenience that was occasioned as a result.

Many female tram drivers were also taken on as temporary replacements for those of the staff called up for active service. As more and more men were drawn into the unfolding tragedy of war, poster campaigns – organised by the Government in an effort to improve recruiting figures – produced a slightly negative effect, with many women openly approaching men in the street and understandably, but perhaps a little unfairly, taunting them for not joining up by presenting them with a white feather as a sign of cowardice. The Government, realising what was happening, were compelled to issue vital war workers, such as drivers and conductors, with special badges to identify them as such.

Sadly the General Manager, Mr W A Luntley, was to lose his life in March 1915, at the early age of 42, as a result of an accident during field exercises with the

After a few years the track-work became corrugated which in turn caused the trams to be noisy and rough riding. This view, taken on the Dudley Road near Pearson Street, shows the rails being built up by applying weld (a process still used on occasion today) and then ground off level to allow smooth and level running. Cliff Brown collection courtesy John Hughes

Another view of rail repairs on the Dudley Road. Cliff Brown collection courtesy John Hughes

Wolverhampton Volunteer Rifle Corps. As a result of this regrettable accident, Mr Charles Owen Silvers MIEE; MInstT. was appointed as the new General Manager, with effect from 1 December 1915.

Zeppelin air raids in 1916 continued to give problems for the Transport Department - they killed 1413 civilians in the country during the course of the war - and in an effort to reduce being seen from the air, instructions were issued to reduce all lighting in tramcars to give just a weak blue light. All cars were instructed to come to a stop during air raids.

The double-track lines on the south-west side of Victoria Square became redundant, and were used for stabling points only, having latterly been required for the Bilston and Tettenhall services. During race days, special shuttle services were worked along the Bushbury route as far as Dunstall Park, which lay adjacent to the main road. The fare for this was 3d single. On occasions such as this, every available car was pressed into service. Fares were nominally 1d per mile, workman's fares being available up to 7.30am, with children up to the age of 12 years travelling at half fare.

The tram rails now in use were one hundred pounds per yard weight, laid on a six-inch bed of concrete. In the town centre, and near to public buildings, wooden blocks surrounded the rails, but elsewhere granite setts were used for the paving. All points were single-tongued with the exception of those in Victoria Square, which were double-tongued. Certain cars developed a symptom of 'horsey stupidity' in as much that numbers 27 and 29 when working along Waterloo Road with the points set for Bushbury, would invariably turn into New Hampton Road East and head for Whitmore Reans!

After many years of bitter fighting and the signing of a formal treaty at 5.00am on the 100th day of the fifth year of fighting, the war finally ended and all hostilities stopped on November 11, significantly, at the eleventh hour, of the eleventh day, of the eleventh month. In the House of Commons that afternoon, the Prime Minister, Lloyd George, spoke, rising to announce the momentous event, with the signing of the cease-fire document and the peace that had finally come.

By the end of the war in 1918, the tramway system generally was in a poor state of repair, with a backlog of maintenance work to complete (there were still a number of open-fronted cars running as late as 1917). A shortage of labour and materials had not helped the situation. Fares were increased, the minimum rising by 1½d, and a proposal put forward that certain sections of single-track route should be upgraded to double track, to cope with the anticipated increase in passenger traffic. Having served its fourteen years guarantee,

A further view of rail repairs on the Dudley Road. Cliff Brown collection courtesy John Hughes

This view was taken in New Cross district, on the Wednesfield Road, in 1922. It shows the tramway tracks and roadway in a much deteriorated condition; it was track-work at its worst, following the deprivations of the First World War, and provided the catalyst for the introduction of trolleybuses on this route in 1923. Cliff Brown collection courtesy John Hughes

a review of the Lorain system was due. It was becoming increasingly difficult to maintain the surface contact equipment, as the company that supplied it had by this time, not surprisingly, gone out of business. Numerous worn out studs were dotted about the system, resulting in poor electrical contact and making daily operations somewhat erratic.

In the end, the Lorain system was to run for a total of twenty years, in the process outlasting several other stud systems, which had a much shorter life in the U.K. Lincoln used the Griffiths-Bedell system from 1905 to 1919, and the Dolter system was used in Mexborough from 1907 to 1908, and Hastings, where it ran from 1907 to 1914.

Female employees clearing the tracks through Princes Square, following a heavy snowfall. Cliff Brown collection courtesy John Hughes

Mr Luntley's grave at Jeffcock Road cemetery, Wolverhampton in May 2010. Author's collection

Women's Volunteer Reserve. Author's collection

CHAPTER 7 Conversion to Overhead Electrification

In October 1919, Charles Owen Silvers submitted a report to the Tramways Committee emphasising the state of the badly-worn track and urgent need for renewal. Much of the existing single track would need doubling to accommodate increased traffic flows. In an effort to avoid problems with future supplies and potential engineering difficulties, he urged that conversion to an overhead system be considered. That said, it was not until June 1920 that the matter was brought before the council. With the current dilemma in mind, urgent discussions were held on the direction that they should now take, the corporation coming to the somewhat uncomfortable conclusion that the way ahead lay with overhead supply. It was evident that the pro-Lorain faction had nowhere to go and the legacy of an isolationist policy over the years was making itself felt.

It fell to Sir Charles Mander (who was created a Baronet for his public services in the Coronation honours of King George V in 1911) to present the proposal to Council, the conversion costs being £375,000. This cannot have sat easily with him in view of his opposition to the idea back in 1901, with the Express & Star newspaper being quick to remind its readers of the fact. There was lively and sometimes bitter debate within the Council Chamber. Heated arguments on both sides lasted upwards of five and a half hours before the Tramways Committee's proposal was finally accepted. In November 1920, Sir Charles Mander was now succeeded as Chairman of the Tramways Committee by Alderman Stephen Craddock JP.

Notwithstanding the above, the possibility of eventual conversion of the tramway system to trolleybus operation was looming ever closer, the Ministry of Transport having given potential manufacturers a boost during 1920 with the relaxation of maximum vehicle weight from five tons loaded to five tons unloaded, thus paving the way for construction of double-deck vehicles. Relief of rates continued to be paid, with the 1920 contribution of £45,154 leaving funds of £85,640 held in reserve.

Six new tramcars were delivered by Dick, Kerr & Co Ltd in the second half of 1920. They were fitted with bodies supplied by the United Electric Car Co Ltd, both companies now part of the newly-formed English Electric Co Ltd. The last cars to be fitted with Lorain equipment, 53-56, were double deckers, whilst 57-58 were of single-deck closed type. The single-deck trams were fitted with trolley poles for dual operation on arrival, the double-deck trams not being fitted until some time later.

Erection of overhead line traction poles commenced on 26 January 1921, with trams able to draw current from the overhead wires as shown below -

Route 8 – Dudley Road .... 26 March
Route 7 – Bilston Road................ 15 June
Route 5 – Willenhall Road .... 22 July
Route 6 – Wednesfield................ 28 July
Route 2 – Whitmore Reans .... 28 August
Route 3 – Bushbury..................... 1 October
Route 1 – Tettenhall................... 5 October
Route 4 – Penn Fields .... 15 October

Cleveland Road depot in 1921. The overhead system has now replaced the Lorain surface contacts. Tracks are about to be installed in the depot extension, built in 1920. Cliff Brown collection courtesy John Hughes

Above: Car 69, one of eight such vehicles delivered by Brush in March 1922, and pictured outside Cleveland Road depot.

Right: A poor quality but very rare picture of a solid-tyred overhead repair lorry in Cleveland Road depot, possibly a Tilling-Stevens TS3.

Below: An interior view of Cleveland Road depot, showing a number of works cars, including A3, the combination track sweeper and snow plough. Cliff Brown collection courtesy John Hughes

Stafford Road, at Gorsebrook Road junction in 1924. On the left are the 'Concrete Cottages'; built in 1876, these extremely strong constructions were demolished (with some difficulty) in 1966. The Gas Works and the Bridge Inn, another building of longevity, are on the right. Cliff Brown collection courtesy John Hughes

The conversion programme was completed by 19 October and carried out using direct labour under the personal direction of the General Manager, Mr Silvers. In the main, work was carried on with manual labour, using blocks and tackle ropes plus wooden shearlegs. Traction poles were delivered by steam wagon and unloaded as required along the length of road being worked on. They were of standard simple design, having a galvanised base and finished off with a finial of ball and rounded spike design. In the town centre, much use was made of rosettes attached to the walls of nearby buildings, thereby reducing the visual impact. In all, approximately 1100 poles and 74 rosettes were used. Span wire suspension was used in the main, bracket arms being provided where single track sections were near to the kerbside. These were fitted with supporting suspension arm stays, but without any of the scroll work common to this period. All poles were painted in a deep mid green, commonly referred to in later years as Corporation Green.

The wiring for Whitmore Reans terminated at Hunter Street, but the triangle at New Hampton Road West was wired up, allowing one place on the system where trams could be completely turned around. Advice was given that the poles were strong enough to carry the extra running wire and tensioning wires required for trolleybus operation, a fact that was later proved in some depth as several of the original traction poles survived in use through to the 1960s. A feature that had not been required in operation of the Lorain system was the tower wagon, for use with overhead repairs and maintenance. Several were now produced with at least one utilising the chassis of an early Tilling-Stevens bus. A reel wagon was also used to assist in stringing up the running wire, done mainly at night so as to minimise disruption to other traffic.

As each route was converted, trams were made available by the simple expedient of fitting a trolley arm and removing the Lorain gear. This allowed lifeguard trays to be moved back to a more conventional location. One downside of the conversion became apparent as the Lorain equipment was progressively removed from the tramcars. The loss of one ton of weight from a low centre point resulted in a tendency in trams to sway and roll at speed and on corners, the Du Pont cars being particularly prone to this.

A view down Victoria Street from Queen Square in 1925. Car 11 is waiting in the loop for the tram ascending Victoria Street. From the overhead wiring, it will be seen that trolleybuses have already taken over on the Bushbury route.

Victoria Street in the early 1920s. By 1928, the property on the left hand side had been demolished and the roadway widened. The motor bus making its way up the hill will soon have to move over as a double-deck tram has just entered from Queen Square. Note the two sets of overhead line, despite the fact that this was a single line section with passing loops at each end.

Penn Fields circa 1923, at the junction of Stubbs Road and Lea Road, looking down Birches Barn Road. Beckminster House can be seen in the left background; there is now a Methodist church there. Outward bound car 59 is about to swing into Stubbs Road and is near the end of its journey. There is now a traffic island at this location, with a row of busy urban shops where the far fence stands.

Images Cliff Brown collection courtesy John Hughes

By Inkerman Street and close to Woden Road, Heath Town, on the Wednesfield Road in 1922. Note the two sets of running wires, perpetuated along the route despite the fact that much of the way was single track with passing loops. The shop on the left with sign above the awnings was an outlet for Viking pedal cycles. A local concern, the Viking Cycle Company had their manufacturing base close to Berry Street in the town centre – Berry Street ran behind the GPO building and the Grand Theatre, from Market Street to Victoria Square.

Snow Hill terminus in the early 1920s; note amount of people walking. In later years, the Gaumont cinema had an additional storey added to the building, making it quite impressive.

Of the 15,000 Lorain studs still in use around the system, 9000 now had redesigned tops which the council had fitted in 1909, leaving about 5000 with improved Lorain tops introduced in 1903; the remainder having the original 1902 type. The Lorain studs were not removed until all other track and road works had been completed, those in Cleveland Road depot being remarkable survivors and remaining in place in the depot floor until the demise of the trolleybus system in March 1967. They were finally removed on demolition of the depot in 1979. An example of the Lorain stud is now on display at the National Tramway Museum, in Crich, Derbyshire.

Following the opening of the Dudley Road section on 26 March 1921 with overhead wiring, WDET trams recommenced running through from Dudley to Snow Hill with the Bilston to Dudley service now being cut back to Fighting Cocks. Meanwhile, corporation cars continued to operate a frequent service, terminating at Fighting Cocks. In the same year improvements were made to sections of single track possessing poor visibility between the passing loops. They were fitted with automatic occupation indicators attached to traction poles at the beginning of the single-track sections; tripped by contacts on the overhead wire, green or red bulbs would light to indicate to motormen if there was section occupancy by other trams.

All double-deck cars were now fitted with new, larger GE249 ventilated motors. Three additional double-deck car bodies were also purchased from English Electric in 1921, making use of existing trucks taken from scrapped single-deck trams. Numbered 59-61, the new cars used the trucks from trams 4,10 and 8 respectively. The trams were similar in style to 53-56, but equipped for trolley collection only and did not receive Lorain equipment.

Eight of the displaced GE60 motors found further use and were fitted to new vestibule cars supplied during 1921 – 1922. Numbered 62-69, these cars had Peckham 8ft 6in trucks, were fitted with front exit bodies supplied by Brush and had no internal bulkheads, the motormen being screened at night by a drawn curtain. To meet the Ministry of Transport requirements, they had side guards and folding steps fitted. The eight cars were of long-wheelbase single-truck all-enclosed design, and these cars also never gained Lorain equipment. At first, the cars were designated non-smoking, rapidly earning the somewhat unkind name of 'The Pussyfoot Fleet'. These last trams to be purchased worked only on the overhead system and thus had a useful working life of less than five years.

It was perhaps a little sad that Wolverhampton's tramway system was reconnected, in the fullest sense of the word, with the rest of the Black Country network, just as a decision was reached to abandon it in favour of

Left: Colour light signals are displayed to good effect here on the Penn Fields route, between Owen Road and Bristol Street. As a result of road curvature and poor visibility for tram drivers, the equipment – designed to advise drivers of track occupation on the single line sections – was installed over the whole length of Lea Road and Stubbs Road, where the route ended with a long length of single track. Note the overhead skate; the passage of a tram boom will trip an indicator light on the adjacent traction pole and one at the other end of the loop.

An official picture of the ornate lining on car 61, done in gold leaf. Cliff Brown collection courtesy John Hughes

Car 61 in Lea Road; possibly an official photograph taken shortly after delivery in 1921. Note that the car is parked up and displays an incorrect number for this route.

A slightly later view of Stubbs Lane, showing how quickly urban development was taking place. The attractive half-timbered houses are still there today and very sought after.

Images Cliff Brown collection courtesy John Hughes

Above: The bad winter of 1925/6 in Portobello, Willenhall.
Cliff Brown collection courtesy John Hughes

the trolleybus. Proposals made at this time to commence through running to Walsall did not come to fruition. In 1922, Cleveland Road depot was again extended westwards to cope with the ever-increasing fleet. Eventually the Corporation purchased the majority of the WDET's routes. For a period of time after the purchase, corporation trams covered some of the services, which with one exception were converted in the fullness of time to trolleybus operation. Over the next five years, the tramway system gradually contracted, as the network was steadily converted to trolleybus. Conversion of the corporation services came in the following order –

Route 6 to Wednesfield	29 October 1923
Route 3 to Fordhouses	9 March 1925 *(extended from Bushbury Lane)*
Route 8 to Fighting Cocks	26 October 1925
Route 5 to Willenhall	16 May 1927 *(Neachells Lane)*
	16 September *(Market Place)*
Route 4 to Penn Fields	16 July 1927
Route 1 to Tettenhall	29 November 1927 *(Wergs Road)*
	1 January 1928 *(Wrottesley Road)*
Route 2 to Whitmore Reans	27 January 1930
Route 7 to Bilston	19 November 1928

A detailed description of the events covering the overlap, leading up to the closure of each route and the opening of a full network of trolleybus routes, can be found in the following pages. Following the final abandonment on 26 August 1928, three double-deck trams were sold to York, almost certainly 55, 56 and 61. Two went in November and one in December, having first been stripped of their top covers, and fitted with trolley poles and standards from open-top cars.

In retrospect, it can be said that adoption of the untried and virtually unknown Lorain system of surface contact collection was a brave but foolhardy attempt by a council seemingly dogged by internal politics and having a 'not in my backyard' attitude to overhead electrification. Despite the proven benefits, they were utterly determined to plough their own furrow. That members of the council were led (and in some cases coerced) by one particular Alderman, intent on dominating the proceedings, cannot be denied. The result was a venture that was inevitably doomed to failure. As to the secondary reason for staying with the system, thereby keeping the BET and its associated companies out of Wolverhampton for many years, to the financial benefit of the council, it is difficult to assess just how much was lost elsewhere to the townspeople in the way of commercial development and investment and the question has to be asked as to whether the town's best interest was served by this action.

Above: Tramway crews' social club in 1926. Arthur Whitehouse

Right: Track deterioration after the end of World War 1. It was this that hastened the eventual conversion of the Wednesfield route to operation by trolleybus. Author's collection

Below: Newhampton Road. Maintenance staff Megger-testing the side feed on a section pillar.
Cliff Brown collection courtesy John Hughes

STEWARTS AND LLOYDS LIMITED

BRITISH STANDARD SPECIFICATION FOR TUBULAR TRAMWAY POLES

(ABRIDGED)

CLASSES.

1. The poles shall be of wrought steel free of all defects, and shall be of four classes :—

Light Pole.
Medium Pole.
Heavy Pole.
Extra-Heavy Pole.

CONSTRUCTION.

2. The poles may be made of three separate sections (sectional poles) swaged together when hot so as to make a perfect joint.

Poles shall be made either by the hot-rolled weldless process or the lap-weld process, of steel of a tensile strength of not less than 24 tons nor more than 42 tons per square inch.

The lap-welded seams in the sections shall be set at an angle of one hundred and twenty degrees (120°) to each other.

OVERALL LENGTH.

3. The overall length of poles shall be thirty-one feet (31 ft.) (all classes), or thirty-three feet (33 ft.) (only medium, heavy and extra-heavy classes).

JOINTS.

4. The length of the telescope joint in the poles shall be eighteen inches (18 in.), and the upper edge of each step shall be chamfered off at an angle of not less than thirty degrees (30°).

C

— 31 —

STEWARTS AND LLOYDS LIMITED

LENGTH OF SECTIONS.

5. The visible length of the sections shall be :—

	31 feet Poles	33 feet Poles
Top section, - - - -	7 feet.	7 feet.
Middle section, - - - -	7 feet.	7 feet.
Bottom section, - - - -	17 feet.	19 feet.

OUTSIDE DIAMETERS.

6. The outside diameters of the four classes of poles shall be as follows:—

Class	Top Section		Middle Section		Bottom Section	
	31 feet Poles	33 feet Poles	31 feet Poles	33 feet Poles	31 feet Poles	33 feet Poles
	inches	inches	inches	inches	inches	inches
Light	5½	—	6½	—	7½	—
Medium	6½	6½	7½	7½	8½	8½
Heavy	7½	7½	8½	8½	9½	9½
Extra-Heavy ...	7½	8½	8½	9½	9½	10½

The variation in diameter shall not exceed $\frac{1}{16}$ inch.

MINIMUM THICKNESS.

7. The minimum thickness of metal in any pole shall be as follows :—

Class	Top Section		Middle Section		Bottom Section	
	31 feet Poles	33 feet Poles	31 feet Poles	33 feet Poles	31 feet Poles	33 feet Poles
	inch	inch	inch	inch	inch	inch
Light	$\frac{9}{32}$	—	$\frac{9}{32}$	—	$\frac{5}{16}$	—
Medium	$\frac{9}{32}$	$\frac{9}{32}$	$\frac{5}{16}$	$\frac{5}{16}$	$\frac{11}{32}$	$\frac{7}{16}$
Heavy	$\frac{5}{16}$	$\frac{5}{16}$	$\frac{11}{32}$	$\frac{3}{8}$	$\frac{13}{32}$	½
Extra-Heavy ...	$\frac{5}{16}$	$\frac{5}{16}$	$\frac{7}{16}$	$\frac{7}{16}$	$\frac{9}{16}$	½

The tolerance shall be 5 per cent under the above thicknesses.

STRAIGHTNESS.

8. The completed poles shall be straight and true over their entire length to within one-quarter of an inch (¼ inch).

— 32 —

STEWARTS AND LLOYDS LIMITED

DROP TEST.

9. Five per cent. (5%) of each class of pole shall, if required, be subjected to the following drop test :—

The pole shall be dropped vertically, butt downwards, three times in succession, from a height of six feet on to a hard wood block six inches thick laid on a concrete foundation. The pole shall withstand this test without showing any signs of telescoping or loosening of joints.

BENDING TESTS.

10. Five per cent. (5%) of each class of pole shall be subjected to the following bending tests :—

The pole shall, in each case, be fixed horizontally and rigidly supported for six feet from the butt, and loaded, as a cantilever, at a point eighteen inches (18 inches) from the top, the load being applied at right angles to the axis of the pole. Upon the application of the following loads, the temporary deflection and permanent set, measured at the point of application of the load, shall not exceed the figures stated in the table.

Class of Pole	Load in lbs. for temporary deflection not exceeding 6 in.	Load in lbs. for permanent set not exceeding ½ in.
Light	750	1000
Medium	1250	1750
Heavy	2000	2500
Extra-Heavy	2750	3250

Note.—The loads given above are the total loads calculated to give the specified temporary deflection and permanent set. This load thus includes the overhanging weight of the pole, and the load actually to be applied for testing purposes is the load given in the table less a proportion of the weight of the pole, this latter being the overhanging weight as determined by a spring-balance.

— 33 —

STEWARTS AND LLOYDS LIMITED

REJECTION.

11. In the event of any pole of the above-mentioned five per cent. (5%) not fulfilling the test requirements, a further five per cent. (5%) shall be subjected to the tests enumerated above. Should any further failure occur, the whole parcel from which the poles have been selected shall be liable to rejection.

Note.—Dimensions and particulars of Tramway Poles have been extracted, by permission, from British Standard Specification No. 8. Copies of this specification can be obtained from the British Standards Institution, 28 Victoria Street, Westminster, London, S.W.1.

BRITISH STANDARD TRAMWAY POLES

To facilitate reference the dimensions of the various classes of poles have been tabulated as follows. The weights are given in the British Standard Specification, but only for information, and are not mandatory.

Length.	Type	Dimensions of Sections			Approximate Weight per Pole	Loads Applied 1′ 6″ from top	
		Bottom inches	Middle inches	Top inches	lbs.	Temporary Deflection not more than 6 inches lbs.	Permanent set not exceeding ½ inch lbs.
31 Feet	Light	7½ × $\frac{5}{16}$	6½ × $\frac{9}{32}$	5½ × $\frac{9}{32}$	700	750	1000
	Medium	8½ × $\frac{11}{32}$	7½ × $\frac{5}{16}$	6½ × $\frac{9}{32}$	872	1250	1750
	Heavy	9½ × $\frac{13}{32}$	8½ × $\frac{11}{32}$	7½ × $\frac{5}{16}$	1130	2000	2500
	Extra-Heavy	9½ × $\frac{9}{16}$	8½ × $\frac{7}{16}$	7½ × $\frac{5}{16}$	1437	2750	3250
33 Feet	Medium	8½ × $\frac{7}{16}$	7½ × $\frac{5}{16}$	6½ × $\frac{9}{32}$	1079	1250	1750
	Heavy	9½ × ½	8½ × $\frac{3}{8}$	7½ × $\frac{5}{16}$	1394	2000	2500
	Extra-Heavy	10½ × ½	9½ × $\frac{7}{16}$	8½ × $\frac{5}{16}$	1607	2750	3250

— 34 —

Tramway Pole specification. Author's collection

CHAPTER 8 Under Two Wires - Replacement of the Trams By Trolleybus

A visit was organised to Birmingham on 16 January 1923 by the Tramways Committee, with a view to inspecting the trolleybus system that Birmingham Corporation had installed on 27 November 1922 to replace the ageing tramcar service to the Nechells district. Having assessed its suitability for Wolverhampton's streets, the committee came away comfortable in the knowledge that they would be recommending a satisfactory alternative to the tramway system then in use.

The General Manager, Charles Owen Silvers, presented a report recommending that rather than reconstructing the tramway track on the Wednesfield route and relaying the single line to double track, it should be converted to trolleybus operation and trialled for its suitability for Wolverhampton's streets. In March the council approved the committee's recommendation, though the need for additional wiring was not specifically discussed or considered. The move to trolleybus was to make Wolverhampton a leader in the field of conversion from trams, being second only to Birmingham and the fourteenth operator overall to install a trolleybus system.

Trams ceased running on the 1¾-mile route from Broad Street to New Street on 23 July 1923 and during the conversion, a motorbus service was substituted. On 29 October the new service commenced. The route ran 2¼ miles to a turning circle in the entrance to Neachells Lane, by the Dog and Partridge public house and just short of Pinfold Bridge, being a short way beyond the original tram terminus. To open the service, six new vehicles were purchased from Tilling-Stevens. Numbered 1 – 6, they were TS6 models fitted with Dodson central entrance forty-seat bodies, re-seated to thirty-six seats in November 1927. These vehicles ran on converted petrol-electric chassis, with the engine and generator removed and electrical traction gear installed.

Until additional wiring was erected in the town centre, the trolleybuses could only reach Cleveland Road Depot by using one trolley boom on the overhead wire and trailing a metal skate on the tram rail to provide an earth return for the current. The service was then trialled for one year. Although the corporation possessed no statutory powers to operate trolleybuses, the Minister of Transport confirmed that if the local authorities affected had no objections, then he would not stand in the way.

With the operation proving to be a complete success, the decision was taken to replace all remaining tram services with trolleybuses. The line to Bushbury was in dire need of conversion as the track was badly worn. The tram route left town via Darlington Street and Waterloo Road but a decision was taken to route the new trolleybus service out by Wulfruna Street and in by North Street and Queen Square. On 19 August 1924, the trams were replaced with a substitute bus service using hired vehicles. Seven more Tilling-Stevens vehicles arrived between 24 January and 14 March 1925 to supplement the trolleybus fleet. Trolleybuses commenced running on 9 March, with the opportunity being taken to extend the route beyond the original tram terminus along Stafford Road to the Vine Inn at Fordhouses, though at that time

Trolleybus 1 stands complete with crew of drivers T Wharton and E Talbot on the corner of New Street, Wednesfield, at the site of the old tram terminus. The new service continued over the canal bridge in the background to a turning circle by the Dog and Partridge public house, at the junction with Neachells Lane, giving a new route length of 2¼ miles. Note the primitive 18-inch spaced wiring

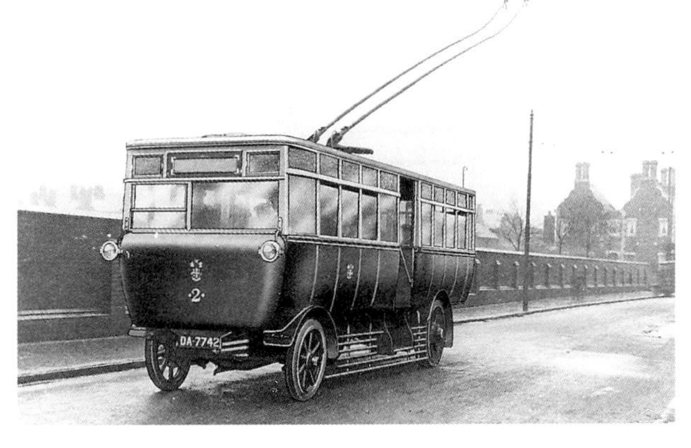

This is a rare publicity shot of trolleybus 2 on the Wednesfield Road, where New Cross Hospital is now located, looking towards Wolverhampton.

Deryk Vernon collection

Above: Queen Square is shown here in the early days of operation in 1925.

Right: The junction of Wulfruna Street and North Street with trolleybus 26, a Tilling-Stevens TS6 supplied 11 November 1926, outbound on route 3A to Fordhouses. The single wiring layout crossed just in front of trolleybus, 26 having earlier travelled in the same direction as the pick-up lorry, making a large anticlockwise circle via Queen Square and Lichfield Street, before regaining Wulfruna Street to commence its journey to Fordhouses.

Author's collection

Trolleybus 11 has arrived outside Cleveland Road depot, after a spell of duty on the Wednesfield route. Deryk Vernon

Trolleybus 22, a Tilling-Stevens TS6, is seen outside Cleveland Road depot. Author's collection

there were few houses in the vicinity.

A short-working loop was installed on the same date at the Greenwood Road turn (adjacent to the Goodyear tyre factory from 1927). A further turning circle was constructed at the junction of Stafford Road and Bushbury Lane where the tram route ended; extra journeys were operated to here from 23 April.

Football traffic at the Molineux Ground was still handled by trams, using the special siding at the North end of Waterloo Road, but after the 1924/5 season trolleybuses and motorbuses dealt with this. In time, the turning circle at Bushbury Lane would be removed as housing development progressed further into the countryside. This now left tram routes to Tettenhall, Willenhall, Whitmore Reans, Bilston, Lea Road, and Fighting Cocks, where route 8 met the WDET tramway from Dudley. On a separate front, following the demise of the South Staffordshire Tramways, the WDET had, on 1 April 1924, taken over all operation of the services between Wednesbury/Walsall and Darlaston/Walsall and Darlaston/Wednesbury, sharing operation of the Walsall services with Walsall Corporation.

During 1924, the Tramways Committee had undertaken negotiations with BET, regarding the operation of trolleybuses on the Dudley route. However, this was complicated by various sections beyond Fighting Cocks being owned by more than one local authority and in one part leased back to the tramway company by Dudley Corporation. After a great deal of negotiation, agreement was reached in principle. It had been intended to transfer ownership on 1 January 1925, but delays in obtaining the necessary powers left the WDET continuing to operate the service whilst receiving a monthly payment from the Corporation.

Royal Assent was given on 7 August for the Wolverhampton Corporation Act 1925, confirming agreement for the purchase of the Fighting Cocks to Dudley section of tramway and granting the corporation powers to operate trolleybuses through to Dudley. At midnight on 14/15 August the corporation took over the routes and depot at Sedgley together with 66 of the WDET company employees. Eight corporation cars were transferred to the depot and six ccompany cars borrowed on a temporary basis. Of the corporation's fleet of double deckers, 15 out of the 35 trams were still running as open-top cars. With the exception of 62-69, all the remaining single-deck cars were fitted with clerestory roofs.

The operation to change over now gathered pace as the line to Fighting Cocks succumbed on 18 August 1925. Seven further trolleys had been ordered from Tilling-Stevens to cover the conversion and were due to arrive in October to operate the new service. On 25 October, following acquisition of the Fighting Cocks to Dudley line from the WDET, trams ceased running between Fighting Cocks and Sedgley. The replacement Sedgley trolley numbered 8A did not start running until all wiring had been completed on 10 November 1926, overhead linesmen having installed trolley wires as far as Sedgley tram depot, the Sedgley – Eve Hill section and tram depot having ceased tram operation on 7 November.

Guy BTX 43 is seen outside Cleveland Road depot shortly after delivery on 29 November 1927. Deryk Vernon

The countryside along this stretch was quite moor-like, at a height of 700 feet and on a natural ridge or plateau, rich in Silurian limestone from which many of the local walls were constructed, with rough grassland dropping gently down to the valley of the Tame in the east where the chimney stacks of the 'black country' rose into the sky like a primordial metal forest. West of the road, the land fell steeply down an escarpment, the Stour valley below revealing a more pastoral scene that cradled the villages of Wombourne and Himley, both served by the Great Western Railway branch from Tettenhall. In all cases of conversion, the intervening time between tram and trolleybus was covered by a substitute motorbus service. The full sequence of conversion was as follows –

Section of route covered	Trams stopped	Trolleybuses started
Snow Hill – Fighting Cocks	18/08/25	26/10/25
Fighting Cocks – Sedgley (Junc: Inn)	25/10/25	10/11/26 (to Bull Ring)
Junction Inn – Eve Hill	7/11/26	11/5/27 (to Sedgley depot)
Eve Hill – Dudley	August 1926	8/7/27 (to Dudley, Stone Street)

Since its inception, the Bushbury/Fordhouses route had, from the Town Hall starting point in North Street, travelled via Queen Square, Lichfield Street, and Wulfruna Street in an anticlockwise direction around St Peter's Collegiate Church and through the northern half of Princes Square. This changed on 22 December 1925 with trolleys running directly via Wulfruna Street, the traffic island at its junction with Stafford Street being provided with a turning circle, thus completing a full circle of wiring with the Wednesfield service already using the island to return down Broad Street.

The General Strike of 1926 was to affect transport services across the country. It commenced on 4 May and at first there was a complete stoppage of work across

An early scene at Penn Fields, after conversion of tram route 4 on 16 July 1927 to trolleybus, as a Guy BTX unloads before swinging around the traffic island and heading back to town.
Author's collection

most of the country. Gradually some semblance of order returned over the ensuing days. In Wolverhampton there was initially a total cessation but by 11 May a motor bus service of sorts was being run by the staff of Guy Motors Ltd, manned by volunteers.

The Wolverhampton Corporation Bill 1925 had sought to establish a through service of trolleybuses between Wolverhampton and Walsall. The Bill was heard concurrently with a Bill promoted by Walsall Corporation seeking powers to operate trolleybuses to Willenhall and by means of a joint working agreement to establish a through service between the two towns. Powers were eventually secured to convert the required lines, though Bilston Urban District Council's rooted opposition successfully blocked conversion of a local tramline. Powers were also obtained for construction of trolleybus routes to Springhill and Aldersley, via Hordern Road. Track on the Willenhall Road was in urgent need of renewal and following a negotiated agreement, the corporation purchased the section between Deans Road and Market Place, Willenhall, from WDET for £6,263. The agreement gave possession on 9 August 1926 when the corporation commenced running a substitute motorbus service, the trams having stopped the previous night.

The ongoing conversion of tram routes to trolleybus had been broadly in line with the General Manager's report to the Transport Committee presented to the council in June 1926 (the Transport Committee had assumed its title in February 1926). In his report, the General Manager had advised that large-scale expenditure would be required to renew the Penn Fields, Tettenhall and Willenhall routes, pointing to the worn-out state of the tram tracks. After some debate it was agreed to convert these routes to trolleybus in the fullness of time, but the Whitmore Reans route was marked down for motorbus operation. Seven more new trolleybuses were destined to enter service during the course of the year.

On 1 December 1926, the corporation took delivery of the first trolleybus to come from Guy Motors. The company had started life in 1914, and were known for flair and innovation, with a wide range of vehicles to their credit. The trolley consisted of a BTX chassis, with Dodson H33/28RO bodywork, and was the first to be fitted with pneumatic tyres, being the only trolleybus in the fleet to have an open staircase. As with all Guy trolleybuses of this period, regenerative braking was fitted, in this instance using a compound-wound motor, incorporating Rees-Stevens type regenerative control. In later years, difficulties with voltage power surges and the potential for damage as a result, would cause this method of braking to fall out of favour, manufacturers reverting to other methods such as hydraulic, air and rheostatic. Given fleet number 33, it entered service on the Sedgley route. Fifteen more of these vehicles were to arrive in 1927 with a further eight in 1928.

Trolleybus services commenced on the Willenhall route from the new starting point in Horseley Fields far as Neachells Lane on 16 May 1927 using single-deck vehicles, being extended to Willenhall town centre on 16 September, where a turning circle was erected at the Market Place. Eventually, this circle was destined to be used by Walsall Corporation for its short workings and as a terminus for the yet to be initiated trolleybus service from Bilston and Fighting Cocks. In December, Walsall corporation did a political about turn, now declaring that the trolleybus was no longer an economic proposition for them, despite their declared intention to the contrary in the Bill promoted in 1925. Wolverhampton Corporation stated that they could not accept this stance and after a lot of hard negotiating on both sides, it was agreed that if receipts reached a required minimum on this route, Walsall would convert to trolleybus.

The Penn Fields section was next in line for conversion, the last tram making its way back to town on the night of Sunday 20 March 1927; the following day saw a motor bus service started between Victoria Square and Duke Street in Penn Fields. By Sunday 27 March 85 men were at work removing track from Queen Square and Victoria Street. A batch of double-deck trolleybuses re-launched the service on 11 July with a turning circle being constructed at the junction of Lea Road and Stubbs Road. This was some three hundred yards short of the old tram terminus at the top of what had been previously known as Stubbs Lane.

On 10 July, the Tettenhall route lost its trams. Though having inaugurated the tram service forty-nine years earlier with horse trams, the corporation chose not to mark the occasion, a feature of their method of operation that was to become all too familiar in later years. After the usual period of motorbus cover, a partial service was instituted to Wergs Road on 29 November, with a full service, turning at an apex to Wrottesley Road starting on 1 January 1928. The terminus lay in the very narrow entrance to Wrottesley Road adjacent to Wergs Road and was soon converted from a reversing triangle into the more familiar turning circle outside the 'Dog and Gun' public house. The opening of the service and journey of the first trolleybus down the route was reported in depth by the town's press, records stating that the event was well received locally, with many people queuing to purchase the 3d ticket and travel through what was still considered to be the elite area of town to Tettenhall terminus.

The removal of trams from the Whitmore Reans service came hard on the heels of the Tettenhall closure, with the service ceasing on 1 October 1927. The following day, a motorbus service began operation to Crowther Road, being extended on 15 October 1928 to form a circular service into Whitmore Reans estate with route 2 operating clockwise via Court Road and route 2A anticlockwise via Hunter Street and Hordern Road. Trolleybuses now operated to Tettenhall, Fordhouses, Penn Fields, Willenhall, Wednesfield and Dudley, leaving just the Bilston area still covered by trams.

Wolverhampton was to play host to the first set of automated traffic lights installed in Britain. They were experimentally connected in Princes Square on Saturday 5 November 1927 and following satisfactory trials, full installation was made in October 1928. A single existing traction pole in the centre of the square was provided with three-aspect lamps hung to face each of the four exits. Below each set of lamps were hung the famous blue enamelled signs bearing the legend 'turning right – keep right'. This became well known for trolleybus drivers endeavouring to turn out of Stafford Street and Broad Street into Lichfield Street, on their way out of town.

Since 1925, an agreement had been sought with the BET company to purchase all remaining tramlines in the Bilston area. This was completed on 9 October 1926, but did not receive Royal Assent until 3 August 1928. The corporation took over some of the lines from the WDET on 27 August with the remainder and Bilston depot coming under their control on 1 September. The corporation-owned tram services had finished on the night of 26 August with car 56 making a last run, through driving rain, from Bilston to Wolverhampton.

The irony was that just five days later, on 1 September, the corporation was to become a tramway owner again, after acquiring the Bilston local services from the WDET. Included in the takeover were the 15 trams based at Bilston depot, the tram depot itself, originally opened in 1900 along with the Grade II listed depot house next door at 34 Mount Pleasant, plus 61 staff, including 18 pairs of drivers and conductors. The trams involved included seven single-deck cars, three double-deck of around 50-seater size and five large double-deck cars, seating around 70 people. They were WDET numbers 9/12/14 -19/25/30/34/102/105/108 and 109, not all of them being placed into immediate service by the corporation. This was supplemented by at least two double-deck corporation cars, which worked the Willenhall to Darlaston service via Bilston, perpetuating the WDET policy of running this route as a through service.

Tramway operation was to last barely three months as each route succumbed to motorbus operation, pending the introduction of trolleybuses, Bilston to Fighting Cocks ending on 25 November, the remaining routes, including Willenhall to Darlaston, ceasing as the last ex-BET tram ran on 30 November, motor buses taking over all services whilst conversion to trolleybus took place. This day saw the closure of both Bilston and Sedgley depots to trams, marking the very end of tramway operation by Wolverhampton Corporation. The changeover was made in piecemeal fashion, and upon conversion, the following sections were reopened for trolleybuses:

Wolverhampton to Bilston 19 November 1928
Bilston to Darlaston 27 May 1929 (as a through route from Wolverhampton)
Whitmore Reans 27 January 1930 (now part of a through service to Darlaston)
Fighting Cocks – Bilston – Willenhall 27 October 1930 (as a through route)

Thus, as 1928 ended, the electric tram finally disappeared from the streets of Wolverhampton, not be seen again for seventy-one years until the summer of 1999 when, with some irony, the ghost of the first electric trams could be felt, as the Midland Metro system made its appearance on the streets of the town, opening, at considerably greater cost than its predecessor, with trams running once more down the original route through Ettingshall, on their way to Bilston and Birmingham.

A Guy trolleybus turns carefully across the Wergs Road at Tettenhall terminus, as a car approaches along the A41, all under the watchful eye of the conductor. The rural nature of this route in the late 1920s and closeness of the terminus to open countryside is quite evident. Author's collection

Tettenhall terminus at the Upper Green, with Guy BTX trolleybus 46 loading passengers prior to turning for the trip back to Wolverhampton. Author's collection

Tramcar Service — **WILLENHALL, BILSTON, DARLASTON ROUTE.**

MONDAYS

		am														pm												
Willenhall	dep	—	—	—	—	--	618	638	then	758	8 8	818	828	838	then	—	158	—	218	then	828	838	848	858	then	1018	1038	1058
Bilston	dep	5 6	530	550	610	—	630	650	every	810	820	830	840	850	every	2 0	210	220	230	every	840	850	9 0	910	every	1030	1050	1110
Darlaston	arr	518	545	6 4	624	—	644	7 3	10	823	833	843	853	9 4	20	213	223	233	243	10	853	9 4	—	924	20	1044	11 4	—
Darlaston	dep	518	545	612	632	—	652	7 3	mins	823	833	843	853	912	mins	213	223	233	243	mins	853	912	—	932	mins	1052	11 5	--
Bilston	dep	530	6 6	628	646	656	7 6	716	until	836	846	9 6	9 6	926	until	226	236	246	256	until	9 6	926	—	946	until	11 6	1117	—
Willenhall	arr	—	618	638	658	7 8	718	728		—	858	918	—	938		238	248	258	3 8		—	938	—	958		—	—	—

TUESDAYS TO FRIDAYS

					am						pm							
Willenhall ...	dep		then	3 58	—	4 18	--	4 38	then	6 58	7 8	7 18	7 28	7 38	then	1018	1038	1058
Bilston ...	dep	as	every	4 10	4 20	4 30	4 40	4 50	every	7 10	7 20	7 30	7 40	7 50	every	1030	1050	1110
Darlaston ...	arr	above	20	4 23	4 33	4 43	4 53	5 3	10	7 23	7 32	7 44	—	8 4	20	1044	11 4	—
Darlaston ...	dep	until	mins	4 23	4 33	4 43	4 53	5 3	mins	7 23	7 32	7 52	—	8 12	mins	1052	11 5	—
Bilston ...	dep	8 38	until	4 36	4 46	4 56	5 6	5 16	until	7 36	7 46	8 6	—	8 26	until	11 6	1117	—
Willenhall ..	arr			4 48	4 58	5 8	5 18	5 28		—	7 58	8 18	—	8 38		—	—	—

SATURDAYS

				am							pm				
Willenhall ...	dep		then	10 58	—	11 18	11 38	—	11 58	then	10 28	10 38	10 48	10 58	11 12
Bilston ...	dep	as	every	11 10	—	11 30	11 50	12 0	12 10	every	10 40	10 50	11 0	11 10	11 24
Darlaston ...	arr	above	20	11 24	--	11 44	12 3	12 13	12 23	10	10 53	11 3	11 13	—	—
Darlaston ...	dep	until	mins	11 32	—	11 52	12 3	12 13	12 23	mins	10 53	11 3	11 13	—	—
Bilston ...	dep	8 38	until	11 46	11 56	12 6	12 16	12 26	12 36	until	11 6	11 16	11 26	—	—
Willenhall ...	arr			11 58	12 8	12 18	12 28	12 38	12 48		—	—	—	—	—

SUNDAYS

		am					pm								
Willenhall ...	dep	—	—	—	9 58	then	5 18	—	5 38	6 0	then	10 15	10 30	10 45	11 0
Bilston ...	dep	9 10	9 30	9 50	1010	every	5 30	5 45	6 0	6 15	every	10 30	10 50	11 0	11 12
Darlaston ...	arr	9 24	9 44	10 4	1024	20	5 44	5 59	6 14	6 29	15	10 44	11 4	—	—
Darlaston ...	dep	9 32	9 52	1012	1032	mins	5 45	6 0	6 15	6 30	mins	10 45	11 5	—	—
Bilston ...	dep	9 46	10 6	1026	1046	until	6 0	6 15	6 30	6 45	until	11 0	11 17	—	—
Willenhall ...	arr	9 58	1018	1038	1058		6 15	6 30	6 45	7 0		—	—	—	—

FARES

	Single	Child
Willenhall to Old Football	1½d. (with next)	1d.
Davis Loop to Bilston Town Hall ...		
Willenhall to Bilston Town Hall"... ...	2d.	1d.
Old Football Ground to Bilston Town Hall	1d. (with next)	1d.
Bilston Town Hall to Loxdale Street ...		
Loxdale Street to Moxley	1d.	1d.
Moxley to Darlaston Bull Stake	1d.	½d.
Bilston Town Hall to Moxley	1½d. (with next)	1d.
Loxdale Street to Darlaston Bull Stake ...		
Bilston Town Hall to Darlaston Bull Stake ...	2d.	1d.

WCT 1928 timetable.

Newly-delivered GUY BTX 33 outside Cleveland Road depot. Note the exposed outside staircase; the only Wolverhampton trolleybus to carry this feature over from the trams they replaced.

Half-way house Tettenhall Road looking towards Newbridge

Author's collection

CHAPTER 9 Working Survivors at the Black Country Living Museum

We are quite fortunate, that several Wolverhampton area trams have survived the cutters' torch to be seen again in the 21st century, with some having been found, in a parlous state, many years after withdrawal. Located at the Black Country Living Museum, cared for by the Transport Group (BCLMTG), they are:

23 – Wolverhampton Tramways Company double-deck horse tram. Built in 1892 at the Falcon Works in Loughborough, now part of the Brush group, it was initially owned by the Wolverhampton Tramways Company, operating on 4ft 8½in tracks. Subsequently taken over by Wolverhampton Corporation, it was withdrawn in 1904 and acquired by a farmer in Seisdon village for a summer house. Subsequently rescued in the 1980s by a group from the museum, it eventually came there in 1998 after being fully restored by horse tram enthusiasts in Southport.

5 – Dudley, Stourbridge & District single-deck tram. The body of this tram also became a summer house in Bennett's Hill, Dudley, after closure of the Stourbridge route in 1930. It was acquired in 1973 and a replacement Brill 21E truck obtained from the Brussels tramway. Once restored, it entered service in 1980 as 5 and having now run for much longer than it did with its original owners. Having recently undergone a complete re-fit, it is now nearing the end of a full restoration programme.

34 – Wolverhampton District Electric Tramways single deck tram. This tram was withdrawn in 1928, shortly after take-over of the Bilston routes by Wolverhampton Corporation. It was sold off together with 102 and both used to form a bungalow in Codsall Wood, near Wolverhampton. Both bodies were eventually recovered when the bungalow was rebuilt, and brought to Dudley; with 102 seen to be in the poorer condition, it became a fixed waiting room at the tram route's southern terminus. Car 34 was fully restored, with another ex-Brussels Brill 21E truck providing the running gear, and it entered service on the museum line in November 1997.

49 – Wolverhampton Corporation double-deck tram. This is the museum's flagship. Following closure of the Penn Fields route in 1927, trams 47 and 49 were purchased and used by an undertaker, Edwin Brown, in Coalbrookdale, by Ironbridge, Shropshire, for an office and timber storage area respectively, being stacked either side of a new main building as gable ends and used as an undertaker's home since 1927 and later a coffin shop. Both bodies were eventually obtained by the Museum from Bill Williams, son-in-law to Edwin Brown, being lifted clear of the site on 23 June 1976 when the house was demolished, and 47, being in poorer overall condition, was then used to assist in the restoration of 49. A surplus 4ft 8½in Brill 21E truck was

Above: The remains of 47 at Dudley in 1989.

Below: Horse tram 23 at the Albion Depot

Author's collection

Tram 34 by Pitts Cottage. Arthur Whitehouse collection

May 2010; tram 34 about to cross the main road and trolleybus wiring. Author's collection

A BET traction pole base, pictured near the village terminus. Author's collection

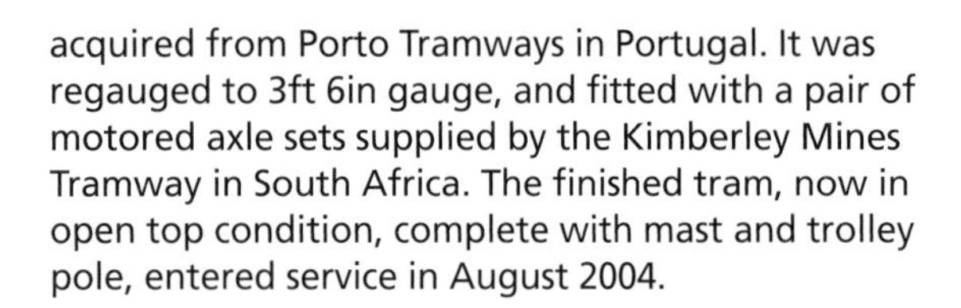

acquired from Porto Tramways in Portugal. It was regauged to 3ft 6in gauge, and fitted with a pair of motored axle sets supplied by the Kimberley Mines Tramway in South Africa. The finished tram, now in open top condition, complete with mast and trolley pole, entered service in August 2004.

Additional to the above are Tividale single-deck trams 75 and 102, which are on site and currently awaiting restoration.

All the trams are located at the Black Country Living Museum, in Dudley, Worcestershire, under the care of the Black Country Living Museum Transport Group (BCLMTG), originally established as the Wolverhampton Trolleybus Preservation Society. The museum began life in April 1976, when work was started on 26 acres of derelict industrial land near the centre of the town. Here you will find one of the finest examples of a working museum in the country, where trams operate a regular service on a lengthy route from one end of the museum complex to the other. Starting alongside the main depot, also home to several trolleybuses, including Wolverhampton 433, that have their own overhead route system, the trams traverse the site, crossing the trolleybus wiring en-route, by the coal mine, and finish at the Albion tram depot, adjacent to the Victorian village, within sight of the Broad Street canal bridge, once the haunt of Wolverhampton trams on route 6 to Wednesfield.

The BCLMTG are responsible for the restoration and crewing of both the trolleybuses (and trams when requested) within the museum site, also the erection and maintenance of all the overhead wiring. A volunteer group, without any Government funding, they have an enviable reputation for the quality of their work, car 49 having won a major award, and they have done much work for other preservation groups within the UK. A visit to this museum is a must for anyone interested in Britain's transport history. There, you can ride on genuine restored trams, in an authentic setting.

The Victorian village, which is continually expanding as candidates become available, was created by rescuing buildings due for demolition, from across the Black Country, dismantling them brick by brick, and carefully rebuilding them at the museum, exactly as they were in their previous location. One of the latest acquisitions is the ex-Cradley Heath Workers Institute, originally opened in 1912 and now fully restored on the museum site.

This has been erected in conjunction with a more ambitious project, the creation of 'Old Birmingham

A view of the beautifully restored lower deck of tram 49.
Arthur Whitehouse collection

Road', an historic High Street of reconstructed shops set in the 1930s, on the opposite bank of the canal to the Victorian village, using an existing road from the Institute to the school building, which lies alongside the tram and trolleybus terminus. The trolleybus route currently runs along the new High Street. Perhaps, one day, the tram terminus could be extended to terminate traditionally, in the middle of the road, opposite Broad Street canal bridge, thus bringing all aspects into one cohesive experience (trolleybus drivers would have to relearn the skills of their predecessors, in weaving around the stationary trams). It is certainly a tantalising prospect and one that deserves to succeed, thus completing the picture of street life in Victorian and Edwardian times.

With the tram route set against the background of the village, complete with its narrow streets and weather-beaten buildings, it greatly enhances the sensation of 'being there' with everything in keeping, as the tram travels past cobbled streets, rocking across the pointwork, with flanges squealing on the tight curves. Familiar signs, such as the tram stops and waiting shelters, are all there ready for the visitor to savour. Now, thankfully, those days gone-by can be revisited, and once more, waiting at the stop, you can –

"Board the Tram"

The bodies of trams 47 and 49 being removed from Ironbridge, Shropshire, prior to restoration. Author's collection

Above: Bill Williams with the remains of trams 47 and 49 at Coalbrookdale in May 1974. Author's collection

Left: Section feeder box awaiting restoration. Author's collection

Below: Night-time operation at the Black Country Living Museum. Car 49 sits outside the main depot. Trolleybuses 433 and 862 can be seen inside the building. Arthur Whitehouse collection

Opposite, top: A view of the upper deck of car 49 at the village terminus. Wolverhampton trolleybus 433 is approaching in the background. Arthur Whitehouse collection

Opposite, bottom: Car 49 is seen in company with WDET car 34 and Manchester trolleybus 1344. Arthur Whitehouse collection

Elkes

PENN FIELDS
TEDDY GRAY
LETTERED ROCK
21 5x
LIMITED STOP
AUDENSHAW
49

Having left the mine stop, car 49 makes its way along the reserved track on the last stage of its journey to the village terminus. Arthur Whitehouse collection

Car 49 is seen at the village terminus with the entrance tracks to the Albion tram depot on the right. Note the adjacent trolleybus wiring. Author's collection

The village terminus. Car 49 waits to depart with a full load, as car 34 prepares to enter the depot. Author's collection

It could be anywhere in the Black Country; car 49 waits quietly in the afternoon sun, by the Albion depot. Author's collection

Wintertime at the BCLM in 2012. The final leg to the village terminus. Author's collection

Left: Launch day of the newly restored Wolverhampton car 49, outside the Albion depot. Trolleybus 433 has arrived to show the two different modes of electric transport, both displaying route 4 to Penn Fields. Author's collection

APPENDIX 1

Fleet List for Wolverhampton Horse Tramways Co

Wolverhampton Tramways Company Limited 1878-1900

Fleet No	Into Service	Type	Builder	Seating
Horse Cars				
1-?	1878	S/ Deck 4-wheel	Stephenson or Hughes	18 or 22
?-20	1878-1879	D/Deck 4-wheel Open Top	Hughes	Unknown
21-24	1892	D/Deck 4-wheel Open Top	Falcon	Unknown
25	1895	D/Deck 4-wheel Open Top	Milnes	Unknown
26	1897	D/Deck 4-wheel Open Top	Unknown	Unknown

N.B. – 'Knifeboard seats' were fitted on double-deck trams up to and including No. 24, subsequent double-deck vehicles having 'garden' seats. By 1890, tram Nos 9, 12-13, 15 and 17 had been withdrawn. Dates for the remainder are unknown.

Above: The competition! Sampson Tharne's horse drawn omnibus outside the 'Rose & Crown' public house in what was then open countryside to the south of Wolverhampton. This is now the Penn Road and within the suburbs; the Rose & Crown still exists, although much changed!

Above, right: A horse tram is approaching Chapel Ash from Newbridge.

Right: A horse tram in Queen Square waiting to depart for Tettenhall.

Author's collection

APPENDIX 2

WCT Tram Routes and Fleet List

Wolverhampton Corporation Tramway Routes

Route No & Initial Lorain Terminus	Opened Lorain System	Opened Overhead System	Closed Tram Service	Through Fare c.1914	Notes
1 Newbridge	12/6/1902	5/10/1921	10/71927	2d	a
2 Coleman Street	1/5/1902	28/08/1921	1/10/1927	1d	b
3 Bushbury Lane	12/8/1904	1/10/1921	19/8/1924	1½d	c
4 Stubbs Lane	10/9/1909	15/10/1921	20/3/1927	1½d	d
5 Coventry Street	2/4/1904	22/7/1921	8/8/1926	1½d	e
6 Church Street	22/6/1904	28/7/1921	23/7/1923	2½d	f
7 Stow Heath Lane	6/2/1902	15/6/1921	26/8/1928	2½d	g
8 Fighting Cocks	8/3/1904	26/3/1921	18/8/1925	1d	h

a At Newbridge, the service passed into Tettenhall Urban District Council. The through fare was initially 2½d. Final terminus was at Tettenhall (Upper Green).

b The through fare applies to the final terminus at Hunter Street. There was one early workmens' service, right through to Tettenhall, via the junction at Newbridge.

c This ran to Bushbury Lane. On race days, there was a special service to Dunstall Park at 3d single fare.

d This was the last route to be laid.

e Single-deck cars used owing to low railway bridge in Horseley Fields. Connected with Wolverhampton District cars at the Willenhall boundary. Through service recommenced 18/04/1906. Final terminus was at the Market Place, in Willenhall.

f Single-deck cars to Wednesfield used, owing to low bridge in Broad Street. Final terminus was adjacent to New Street.

g Connected at Bilston boundary with Wolverhampton District overhead cars. Through service recommenced 09/11/1905. Final terminus was at Lichfield Street, Bilston.

h Connected at Fighting Cocks with Wolverhampton District Electric Traction overhead cars. Through service recommenced October 1906.

Car 32 in 1915, outside C Walsh Graham's timber yard in Wolverhampton. Author's collection

Wolverhampton Corporation Electric Tram Fleet List

Fleet No	Into Service	Body Type	Maker	Truck	Electrics	Seating
1	5/1902	S/Deck Closed	ERTCW	Brill 21E	Dick, Kerr	26
2	5/1902	S/Deck Open Combination	ERTCW	Brill 21E	Dick, Kerr	18/8
3	5/1902	D/Deck Open-top	ERTCW	Brill 21E	Dick, Kerr	22/16
4	5/1902	S/Deck Open Combination	Milnes	Lorain/ Du Pont	B.T.H.	16/16
5	5/1902	S/Deck Closed	Milnes	Lorain/ Du Pont	B.T.H	26
6	5/1902	D/Deck Open-top	Milnes	Lorain/ Du Pont	B.T.H	26/22
7	5/1902	S/Deck Open Combination	Milnes	Brill 21E	Westinghouse	16/16
8	5/1902	S/Deck Closed	Milnes	Brill 21E	Westinghouse	26
9	5/1902	D/Deck Open-top	Milnes	Brill 21E	Westinghouse	26/22
10	2/1902	S/Deck Open Combination	Milnes	Lorain/ Du Pont	Lorain	16/16
11	2/1902	D/Deck Open-top	Milnes	Lorain/ Du Pont	Lorain	26/22
12	2/1902	S/Deck Closed	Milnes	Lorain/ Du Pont	Lorain	26
13-18	Jul/Aug 1902	D/Deck Open-top	Milnes	Lorain/ Du Pont	Lorain	26/22
19-24	Aug/Oct 1902	D/Deck Open-top	ERTCW	Lorain/ Du Pont	Dick, Kerr	26/22
25-30	Early 1904	D/Deck Open-top	Milnes	Brill 21E	B.T.H.	29/22
31-36	Mid 1905	D/Deck Open-top	U.E.C.	Brill 21E	B.T.H.	29/22
37-40	Mid 1905	S/Deck Closed Combination	U.E.C.	Brill 21E	B.T.H.	12/18
41-43	Late 1906	S/Deck Closed Combination	U.E.C.	Brill 21E	B.T.H.	12/18
44-46	1908/9	D/Deck Open-top	U.E.C.	Brill 21E	B.T.H.	29/22
47-49	1909	D/Deck Open-top	Milnes/U.E.C.	Brill 21E	B.T.H.	29/22
50-52	1913	D/Deck Top-covered Open Canopy	ERTCW	Brill 21E	Dick, Kerr	29/22
53-56	c. Sept 1920	D/Deck Top-covered Open Canopy	E.E.C.	Brill 21E	E.E.C.	31/32
57-58	c. Dec 1920	S/Deck Closed Combination	E.E.C.	Brill 21E	E.E.C.	30
59-60	1921	D/Deck Top-covered Open Canopy	E.E.C.	Lorain/Du Pont 59/50	E.E.C.	31/22
61	1921	D/Deck Top-covered Open Canopy	E.E.C.	Brill 21E	E.E.C.	31/22
62-69	c. Mar 1922	S/Deck Closed Front entrance Vestibuled	Brush	Peckham P22	B.T.H.	32

NOTES ON TRAMCARS

All cars were 4-wheel and fleet list seating figures are shown as:
Combination Cars - inside/outside and Double Deck Cars - upper deck/lower deck

Nos 11, 13-18. These were later top-covered.

Nos 13-24. These trams were fitted with and retained their reversed staircases.

Nos 25-36 and 44-49. Reversed staircases replaced by direct spiral staircases.

Nos 1-43. Vestibuled by 1917.

Nos 44-49. Top-covered and vestibuled by 1917.

No 46. This car was unique in being repainted pale green and primrose in 1924.

Nos 4, 8, 10. These cars were never converted to overhead collection and their bodies scrapped in 1921. The trucks fitted to 59, 61 and 60 respectively.

Nos 55, 56, 61. After the final abandonment on 26 August 1928 these cars were stripped of their top covers, then fitted with trolley poles and standards from open top cars, before being sold to York for further service.

N.B. - Certain trams were retrospectively fitted with trolley booms and the necessary
associated equipment to enable them to work under overhead wiring and over routes then operated by the Wolverhampton District Tramways Company.

Nos 19-28 1905 (Side fitted)
Nos 1, 5, 7, 10, 37-40 1906

With the conversion to overhead supply in 1921, all trams were converted to overhead collection, with the exception of 4, 8 and 10, which were scrapped.

Most of the cars then in service (1-49) were vestibuled between 1911 and 1915.

Permanent Way Cars and Road Vehicles

Fleet No	Into Service	Function	Maker	Truck	Electrics
A1	1902/3	Snow Plough/Track Sweeper & Waterer	Dick, Kerr	Brill 21E modified	Dick, Kerr
A2	1903/4	Salt Tender & Track Sweeper	Milnes	Unknown	Dick, Kerr
A3	1907	Track Sweeper & Snow Plough		Mountain & Gibson Rigid Frame	B.T.H.
-	1923/8	Track Welding Wagon. Ex-bus No 1	Albion		

Tramcar Withdrawals and Disposals where known

Fleet No	Withdrawn	Disposal	Use	Notes
1	July 1923	Unknown		
4	1921	'Peacehaven', Billy Buns Lane, Wombourne	Rebuilt as house	Burnt out 7/8/1953
8	1921	Unknown		
10	October 1921	Unknown Kingswood Shropshire	Sports Pavilion	
12	July 1923	Unknown		
17	Unknown	'Breeze', The Bungalow, Lawley, Shropshire	Shed	Gone by 6/1961
32	1924	A V, Lewis London E12	Unknown	Body only
47	1927	Mr Williams, Coalbrookdale, Shropshire	Bungalow	Gone by 23/6/1976 see note A
49	1927	Mr Williams, Coalbrookdale, Shropshire	Bungalow	Gone by 23/6/1976 see note A
52	Unknown	Mrs Whele, The Little Round Hill, Tinkers Castle Road, Seisdon	Fowl House	Top and bottom separate Still extant 20/4/1967
53	Unknown	To Ryton village in Shropshire	Workshop (lower deck only)	Gone by 5/1961
54	26/8/1928	Unknown		
55	26/8/1928	York Corporation	Tramcar (top cover removed)	Fitted with poles and standards
56	26/8/1928	York Corporation	Tramcar (top cover removed)	Fitted with poles and standards
54	Circa 1928	The Poultry Farm, Bratch Road, Wombourne	Storehouse (top deck)	No trace by 5/1961
57	Unknown	Fighting Cocks, adj, present site Parkfield Secondary Modern School	Greenhouse	Cut up 1956/7
61	26/8/1928	York Corporation	Tramcar (top cover removed)	Fitted with poles and standards
62	August 1926	Langley Road, Merry Hill, Wolverhampton	Unknown	Cut up 1965
63	August 1926	Unknown		
64	August 1926	Unknown		
65	August 1926	Maple Leaf Farm	Chicken House	Gone by 1961
66	August 1926	Unknown		
67	August 1926	Unknown		
68	August 1926	Maple Leaf Farm	Chicken House	Gone by 1961
69	August 1926	Unknown		

Note A – Cars 47 and 49 eventually finished up in the hands of an undertaker in Ironbridge, Shropshire, before being repatriated to the Black Country Living Museum (see information on survivors).

Additionally, the following is known:

A tramway frame finished up at the works of Marrey & Son, Railway Lane, Willenhall, as a footbridge.

The top deck of an unidentified tram went to a Mr Sheward of Little Dawley, Shropshire, to be used as a chaff store, this item being cut up by 1964.

A school in Dawley, Shropshire, obtained an open top double decker for an unknown purpose, it was broken up in the 1940s.

Queen Square. Author's collection

Seen here on 13 December 1952 is the inside of tram 4, a Milnes single deck obtained in May 1902 and withdrawn in 1921. As a private residence, known as 'Peacehaven', it was located in Billy Buns Lane, in the village of Wombourne, just outside of Wolverhampton. Rebuilt as a house, it was sadly burnt out on 7 August 1953. Author's collection

Car 47 at Penn Fields in 1920.
Cliff Brown collection courtesy of John Hughes.

APPENDIX 3

Trolleybuses introduced from 1923 until closure of the tramway system in 1928

N.B. – Standard P.S.V. Circle body codes are used as follows: -

Before the seating capacity
B Single-decker
H Highbridge double-decker
UH Utility Highbridge double-decker

After the seating capacity
C Central entrance
R Rear entrance
D Dual entrance/exit
RO Rear entrance with outside stairs

Fleet Nos	Into Service	Delicensed	Chassis	Registration Numbers
1 – 6	29/10/23	24/3/34	Tilling Stevens TS6 Nos 2991/3034-8 Body - Dodson B40C	DA 7741-6
7	23/8/24	31/10/34	Tilling Stevens TS6 No 4501 Body - Dodson B36C	DA 8814
8 – 14	8 24/1/25 9 17/1/25 10 28/2/25 11 16/3/25 12 11/3/25 13 10/3/25 14 14/3/25	31/8/35 31/10/35 31/5/37 30/6/36 31/12/35 31/8/35 31/12/35	Tilling-Stevens TS6 Nos 4502/4/3/5/7/8/6 Body – Dodson B36C	DA 9008-14
15 – 21	15 26/10/25 16 26/10/25 17 27/10/25 18 26/10/25 19 27/10/25 20 29/10/25 21 09/11/25	31/10/34 31/8/35 1/11/35 30/6/36 31/5/37 31/10/34 31/5/37	Tilling-Stevens TS6 Nos 4509-14/7 Body – Dodson B36C	UK 615-21
22 – 32	22 4/6/27 23 6/3/26 24 4/6/27 25 11/11/26 26 11/11/26 27 11/11/26 28 11/11/26 29 12/11/26 30 28/5/27 31 3/6/27 32 17/2/26	31/10/34 31/8/35 30/9/34 31/10/34 31/5/37 29/2/36 31/5/37 31/5/37 31/5/37 6/3/36 31/10/34	Tilling-Stevens TS6 Nos 15/6/22/18/9/21/5/0/4/3/6 Body – Dodson B36C	UK 622-32
33	2/12/26	31/10/36	Guy BTX No 22131 Body – Dodson H33/28RO	UK 633

Fleet Nos	Into Service		Delicensed	Chassis	Registration Numbers
34 – 40	34	8/7/27	28/2/38	Guy BTX	UK 634-40
	35	11/7/27	28/2/38	Nos 22415/8/25/6/4/19/4	
	36	15/7/27	28/2/38	Body – Dodson H33/28R	
	37	11/2/27	28/2/38		
	38	10/9/27	30/11/37		
	39	17/8/27	30/11/37		
	40	19/9/27	30/11/37		
41 – 56	41	6/10/27	28/2/38	Guy BTX	UK 3941/2
	42	24/9/27	30/11/37	Nos 22416/7/665/4/77/81	UK 4243-50
	43	29/11/27	30/11/37	22676/8/98/23078/9	UK 5951-56
	44	8/12/27	30/11/37	23080/77/81/75/6	
	45	1/12/27	28/2/38	Body – Dodson H33/28R	
	46	3/12/27	30/9/38		
	47	9/12/27	30/9/38		
	48	16/12/27	30/9/38		
	49	4/1/28	30/9/38		
	50	19/11/28	30/9/38		
	51	19/11/28	30/9/38		
	52	17/11/28	26/8/38		
	53	17/11/28	26/8/38		
	54	19/11/28	30/9/38		
	55	17/11/28	30/9/38		
	56	23/11/28	30/9/38		

Tilling-Stevens No 10 outside the Town Hall in North Street. It is seen on the original and short-lived anticlockwise town centre loop via Queen Square. Author's collection

APPENDIX 4

Drawings and specifications

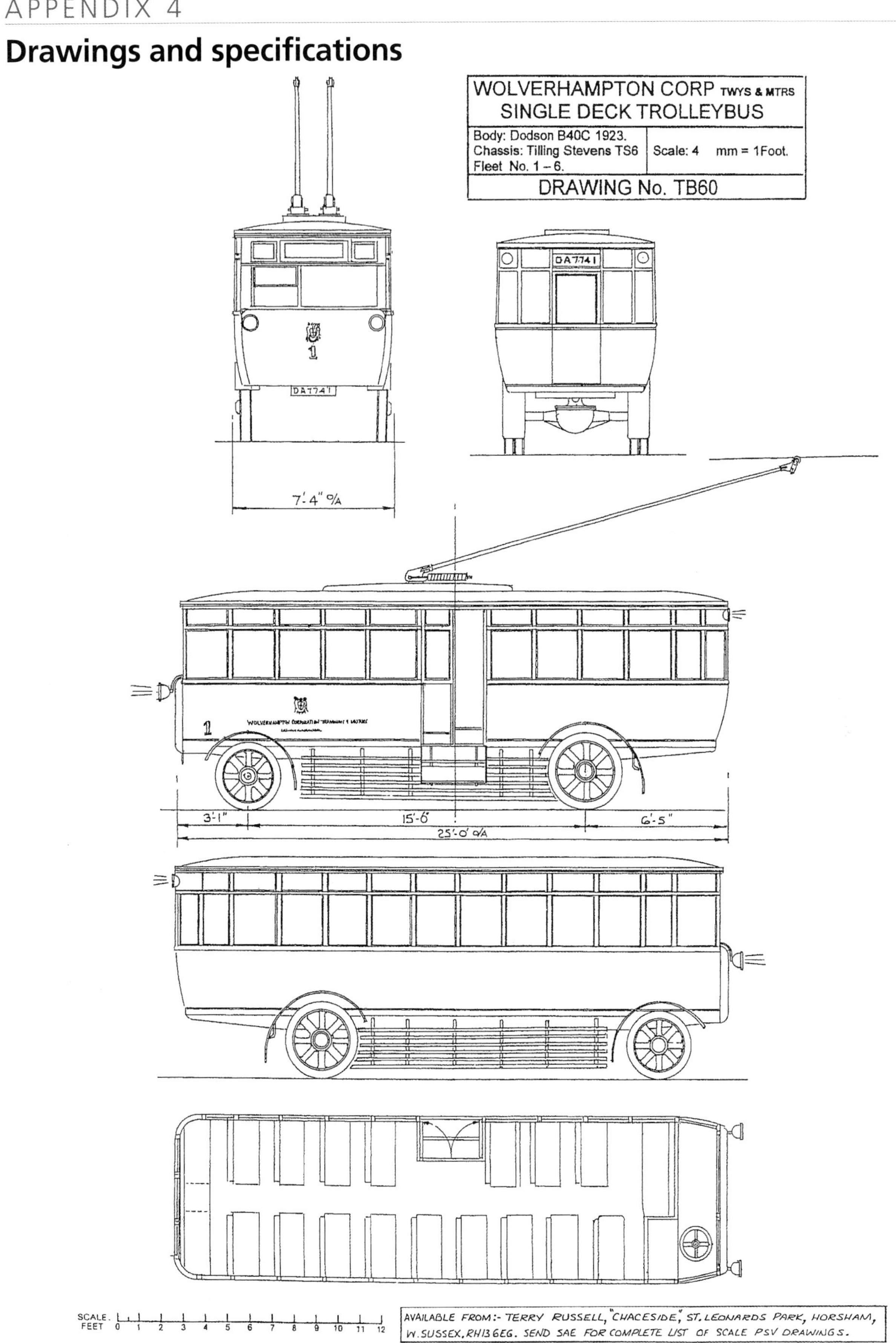

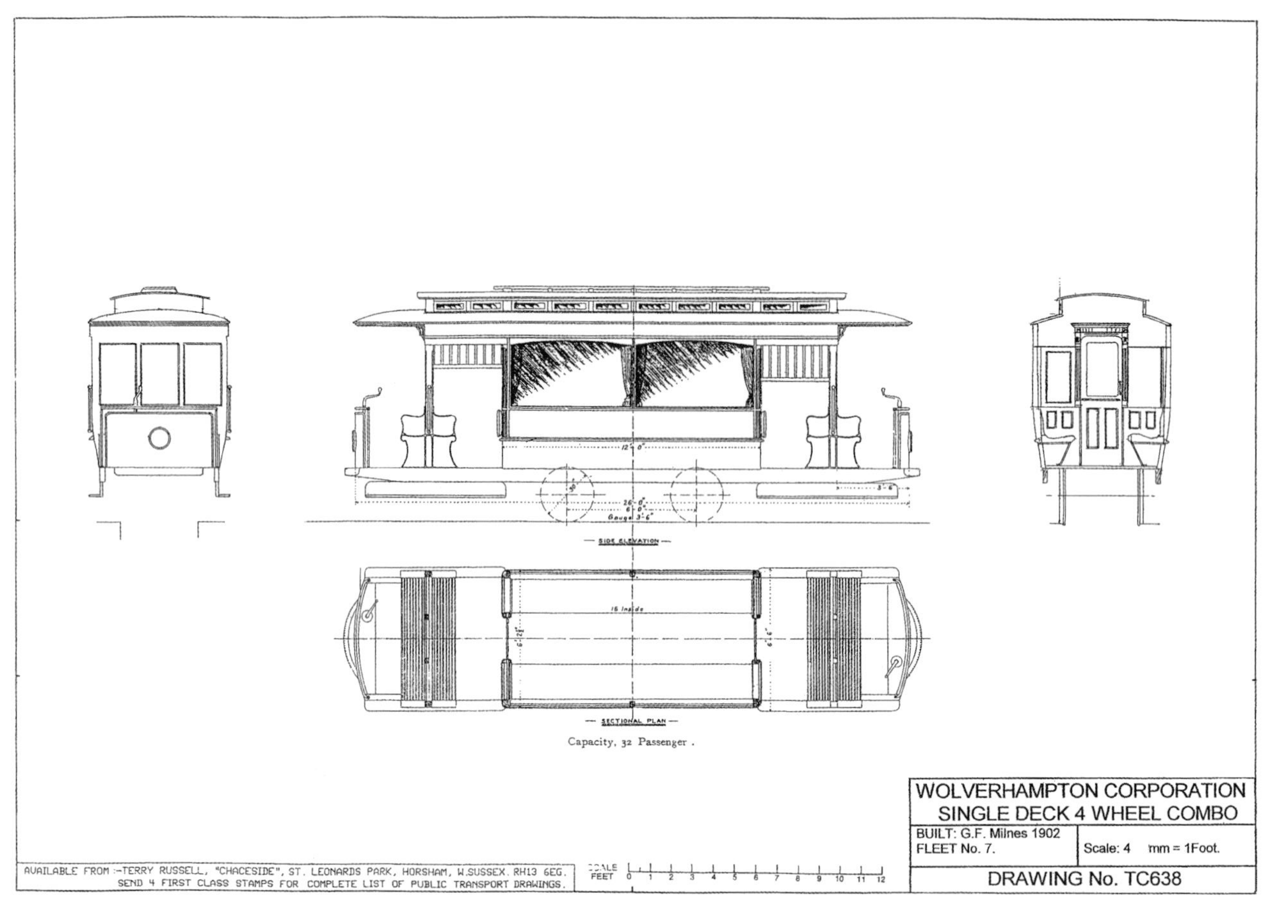
SIDE ELEVATION
SECTIONAL PLAN
Capacity, 32 Passenger.
WOLVERHAMPTON CORPORATION
SINGLE DECK 4 WHEEL COMBO
BUILT: G.F. Milnes 1902
FLEET No. 7.
Scale: 4 mm = 1Foot.
DRAWING No. TC638
AVAILABLE FROM :-TERRY RUSSELL, "CHACESIDE", ST. LEONARDS PARK, HORSHAM, W.SUSSEX. RH13 6EG.
SEND 4 FIRST CLASS STAMPS FOR COMPLETE LIST OF PUBLIC TRANSPORT DRAWINGS.
SCALE FEET 0 1 2 3 4 5 6 7 8 9 10 11 12

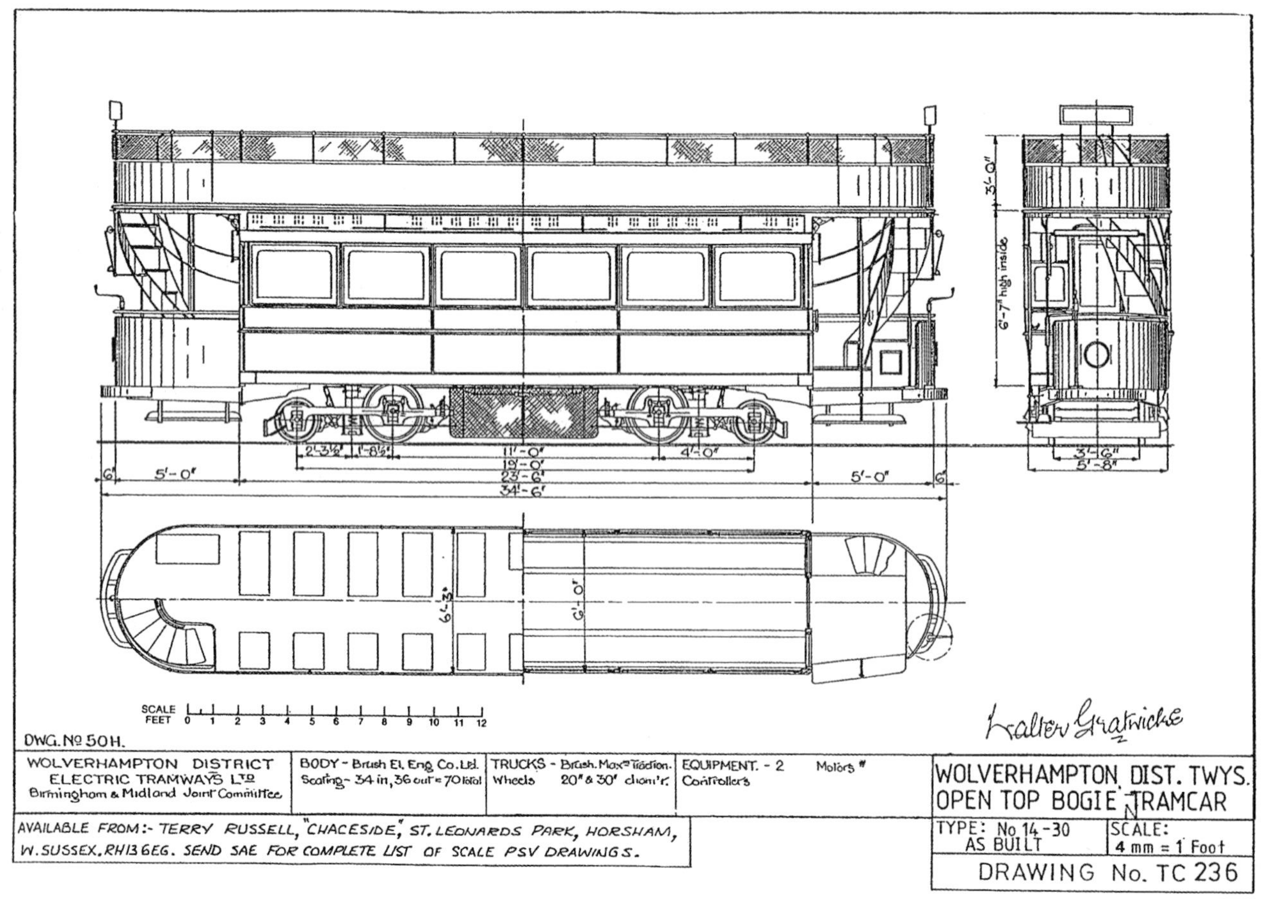
3'-0"
6'-7" high inside
5'-0"
11'-0"
19'-0"
23'-6"
34'-6"
4'-0"
3'-6"
5'-8"
6'-0"
SCALE FEET 0 1 2 3 4 5 6 7 8 9 10 11 12
DWG. No 50H.
Walter Gratwicke
WOLVERHAMPTON DISTRICT ELECTRIC TRAMWAYS LTD
Birmingham & Midland Joint Committee
BODY - Brush El. Eng. Co. Ltd.
Seating - 34 in, 36 out = 70 total
TRUCKS - Brush. Maxm Traction.
Wheels 20" & 30" diam'r.
EQUIPMENT. - 2 Motors
Controllers
WOLVERHAMPTON DIST. TWYS.
OPEN TOP BOGIE TRAMCAR
TYPE: No 14-30 AS BUILT
SCALE: 4 mm = 1 Foot
DRAWING No. TC 236
AVAILABLE FROM:- TERRY RUSSELL, "CHACESIDE", ST. LEONARDS PARK, HORSHAM,
W.SUSSEX. RH13 6EG. SEND SAE FOR COMPLETE LIST OF SCALE PSV DRAWINGS.

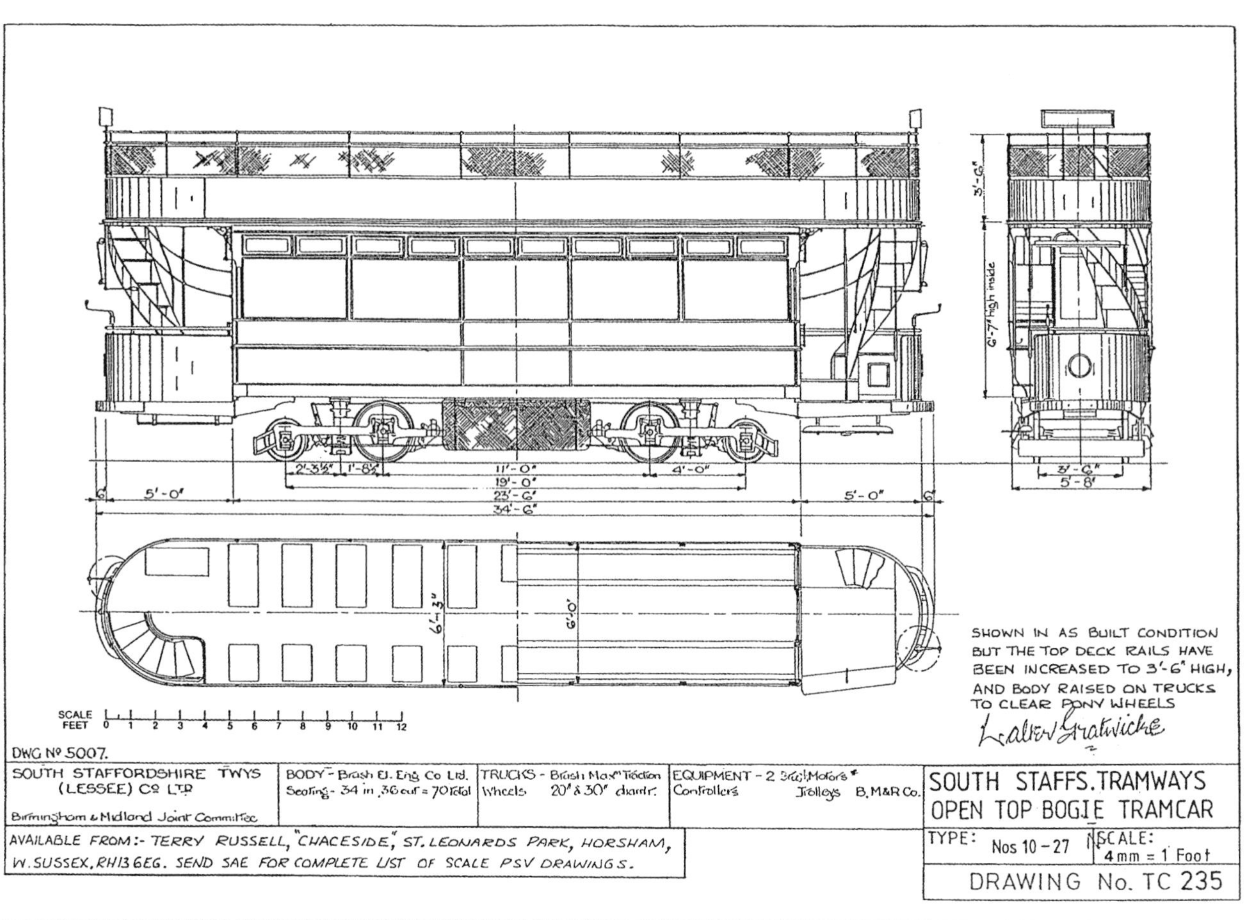
3'-6"
6'-7" high inside
2'-3½"
1'-8½"
11'-0"
19'-0"
23'-6"
34'-6"
4'-0"
5'-0"
6"
3'-6"
5'-8"
6'-3"
6'-0"
SHOWN IN AS BUILT CONDITION BUT THE TOP DECK RAILS HAVE BEEN INCREASED TO 3'-6" HIGH, AND BODY RAISED ON TRUCKS TO CLEAR PONY WHEELS
Walter Gratwicke
SCALE FEET 0 1 2 3 4 5 6 7 8 9 10 11 12
DWG No 5007.
SOUTH STAFFORDSHIRE TWYS (LESSEE) Co LTD
Birmingham & Midland Joint Committee
BODY - Brush El. Eng Co Ltd. Seating - 34 in, 36 out = 70 total
TRUCKS - Brush Maxm Traction Wheels 20" & 30" diamr.
EQUIPMENT - 2 Motors Controllers Trolleys B, M&R Co.
SOUTH STAFFS. TRAMWAYS
OPEN TOP BOGIE TRAMCAR
TYPE: Nos 10 - 27
SCALE: 4 mm = 1 Foot
DRAWING No. TC 235
AVAILABLE FROM:- TERRY RUSSELL, "CHACESIDE", ST. LEONARDS PARK, HORSHAM, W. SUSSEX. RH13 6EG. SEND SAE FOR COMPLETE LIST OF SCALE PSV DRAWINGS.

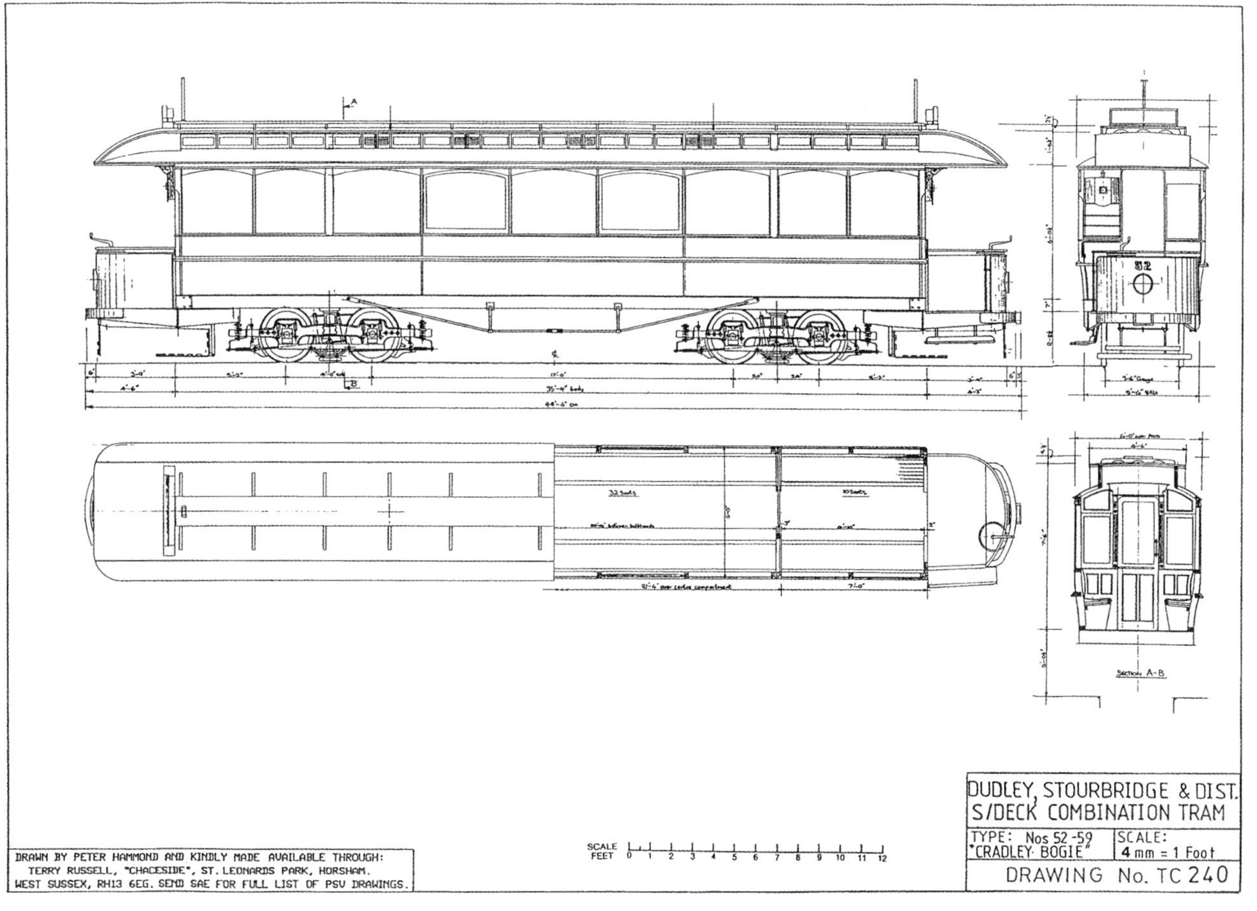
Section A-B
SCALE FEET 0 1 2 3 4 5 6 7 8 9 10 11 12
DUDLEY, STOURBRIDGE & DIST.
S/DECK COMBINATION TRAM
TYPE: Nos 52-59 "CRADLEY BOGIE"
SCALE: 4 mm = 1 Foot
DRAWING No. TC 240
DRAWN BY PETER HAMMOND AND KINDLY MADE AVAILABLE THROUGH:
TERRY RUSSELL, "CHACESIDE", ST. LEONARDS PARK, HORSHAM.
WEST SUSSEX, RH13 6EG. SEND SAE FOR FULL LIST OF PSV DRAWINGS.

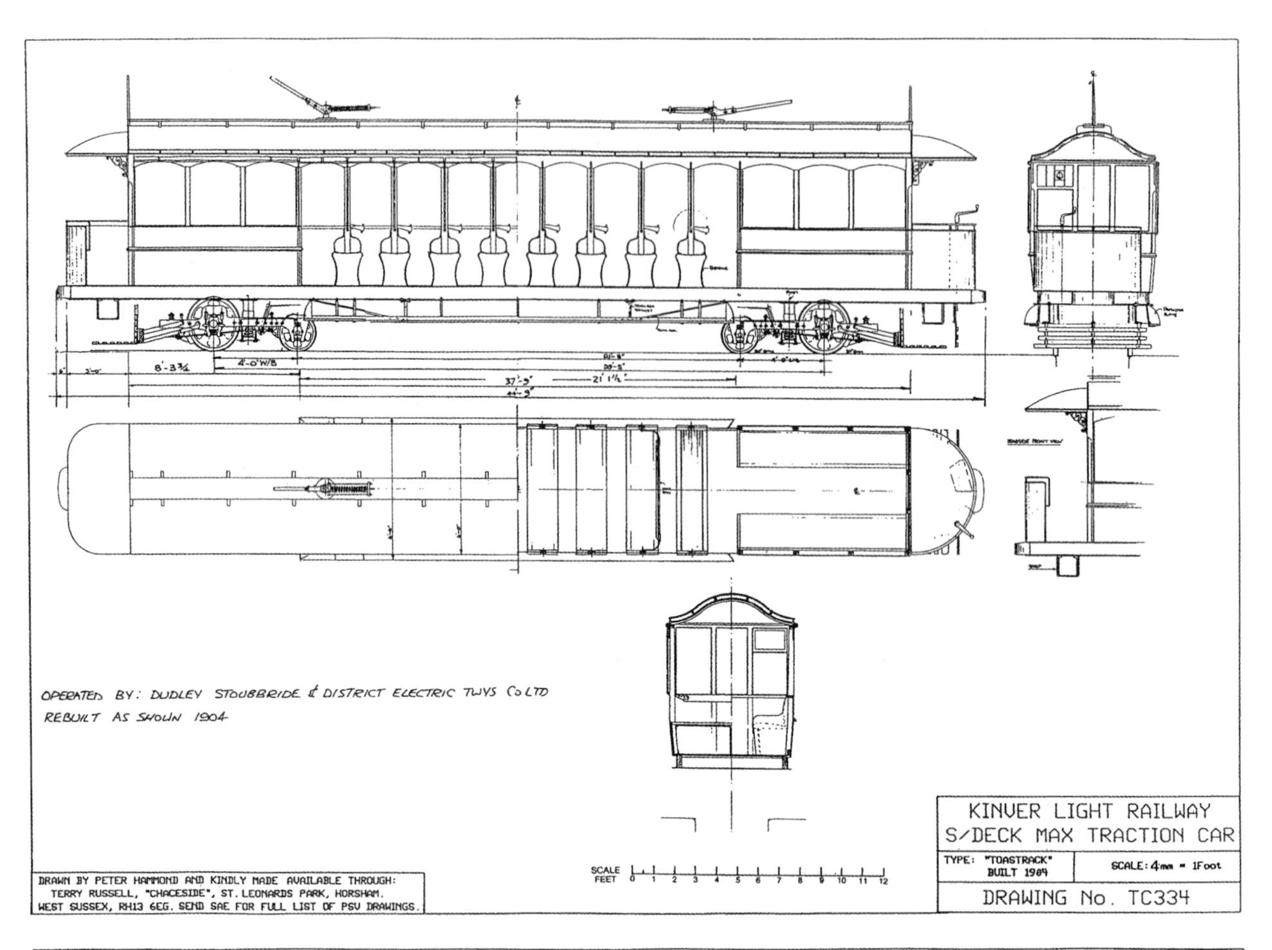
8'-3½
4'-0"WB
37'-5"
21' 1½"
44'-9"
OPERATED BY: DUDLEY STOURBRIDGE & DISTRICT ELECTRIC TWYS CO LTD
REBUILT AS SHOWN 1904
KINVER LIGHT RAILWAY
S/DECK MAX TRACTION CAR
TYPE: "TOASTRACK" BUILT 1904
SCALE: 4mm = 1Foot
DRAWING No. TC334
SCALE FEET 0 1 2 3 4 5 6 7 8 9 10 11 12
DRAWN BY PETER HAMMOND AND KINDLY MADE AVAILABLE THROUGH: TERRY RUSSELL, "CHACESIDE", ST. LEONARDS PARK, HORSHAM. WEST SUSSEX, RH13 6EG. SEND SAE FOR FULL LIST OF PSV DRAWINGS.

Cap
Cone
Straight-line Insulator
Single Pull-off
Double Pull-off
Bracket-arm Insulator
—Various Types of Mechanical Ears
—Globe "Strain" Insulator and Details
TAYLORS PATENT CASTER TROLLEY HEAD
—Winged and Deep-groove Ears
—TROLLEY EAR.
—Double West-End Hanger
—Single Giant Pull-over
—BRACKET-ARM CONSTRUCTION
SECTION OF EAR.
BRACKET-ARM HANGER.
—Double Anchor or "Strain" Ear
Philadelphia Sleeve
Trolley-wire Splicing Sleeve
—Types of Feeder Ears
—Two Types of Splicing Ears
—1, 2, Straight Line. 3, 4, Single Pull-off. 5, 6, Double Pull-off. 7, Bracket Hanger. 8, 9, 10, Bridge and Car Barn Hangers.
Double West-End Pull-off for Points of Extra Stress
—Anchor or "Strain" Ear
—Section of West-End Hanger
—Straight-Line Hanger
—"PRESCOT TROLLEY WHEEL.
TRAMWAY OVERHEAD FITTINGS
DRAWING No. TC454 SHEET 1 OF 2.
AVAILABLE FROM:-TERRY RUSSELL, "CHACESIDE", ST LEONARDS PARK, HORSHAM, W.SUSSEX. RH13 6EG. SEND SAE FOR COMPLETE LIST OF PSV DRAWINGS.

B.I. TRAMWAY POLES AND FITTINGS.
Suitable for Colliery and other Private Lines.

BRITISH INSULATED
:: CABLES LIMITED ::

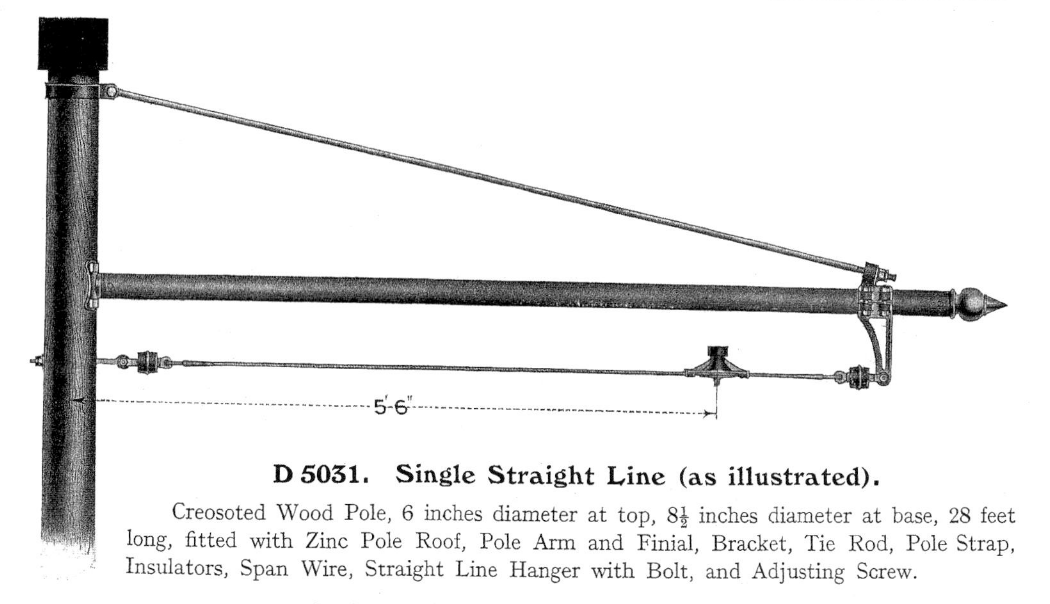

D 5031. Single Straight Line (as illustrated).

Creosoted Wood Pole, 6 inches diameter at top, 8½ inches diameter at base, 28 feet long, fitted with Zinc Pole Roof, Pole Arm and Finial, Bracket, Tie Rod, Pole Strap, Insulators, Span Wire, Straight Line Hanger with Bolt, and Adjusting Screw.

D 5032. Double Straight Line.

As **D 5031,** but with extra Straight Line Hanger and Bolt.

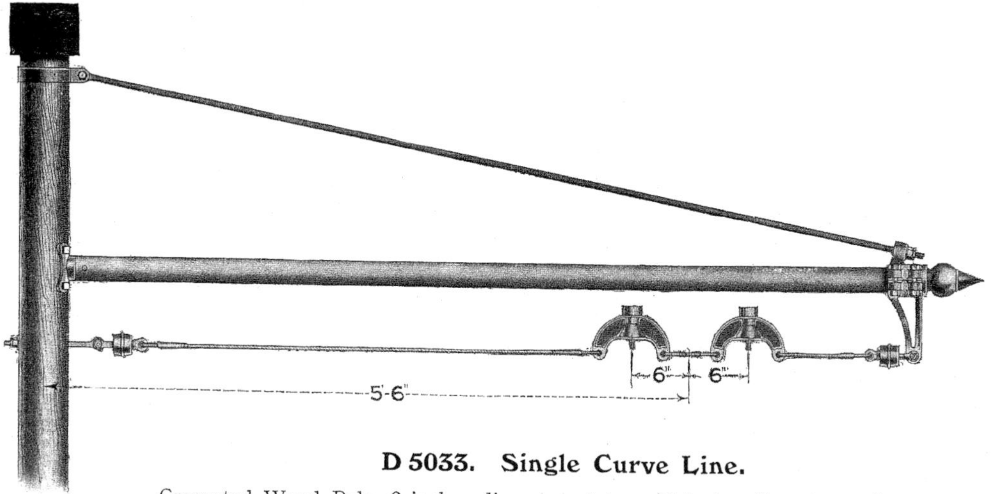

D 5033. Single Curve Line.

Creosoted Wood Pole, 6 inches diameter at top, 8½ inches diameter at base, and 28 feet long, fitted with Zinc Pole Roof, Pole Arm and Finial, Bracket, Tie Rod, Pole Strap, Insulators, Span Wire, Curve Hanger with Bolt, and Adjusting Screw.

D 5034. Double Curve Line (as illustrated).

As **D 5033,** but with extra Curve Hanger and Bolt.

If poles of dimensions different from the standard are required, please state full particulars.

4

WOOD STRAIN INSULATORS

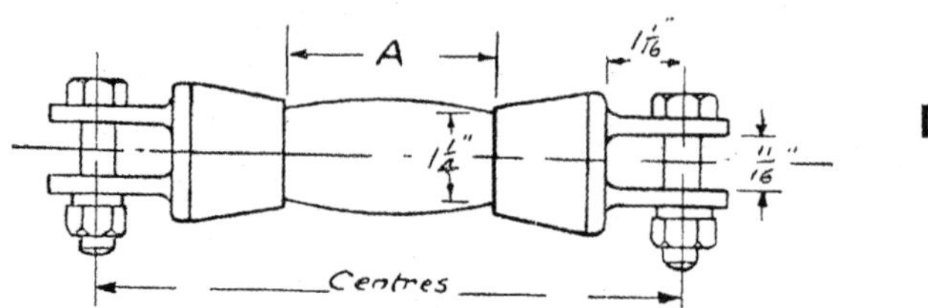

Double Clevis Type

A inch	Length of Wood	Centres inch	Weight lb.	Part No.
3	$5\frac{3}{4}$	$8\frac{3}{8}$	3.10	AA 90-260 Fig. 1
5	$7\frac{3}{4}$	$10\frac{3}{8}$	3.20	,, ,, ,, 2
7	$9\frac{3}{4}$	$12\frac{3}{8}$	3.30	,, ,, ,, 3
9	$11\frac{3}{4}$	$14\frac{3}{8}$	3.37	,, ,, ,, 4
$11\frac{5}{8}$	$14\frac{3}{8}$	17	3.50	,, ,, ,, 5
$12\frac{5}{8}$	$15\frac{3}{8}$	18	3.54	,, ,, ,, 6
$10\frac{5}{8}$	$13\frac{3}{8}$	16	3.48	,, ,, ,, 7

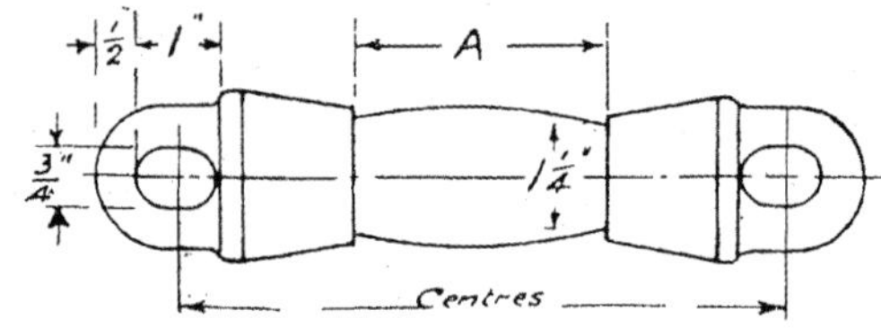

Double Eye Type

A inch	Length of Wood	Centres inch	Weight lb.	Part No.
3	$5\frac{3}{4}$	$7\frac{1}{4}$	2.34	AA 90-261 Fig. 1
5	$7\frac{3}{4}$	$9\frac{1}{4}$	2.43	,, ,, ,, 2
7	$9\frac{3}{4}$	$11\frac{1}{4}$	2.53	,, ,, ,, 3
9	$11\frac{3}{4}$	$13\frac{1}{4}$	2.62	,, ,, ,, 4

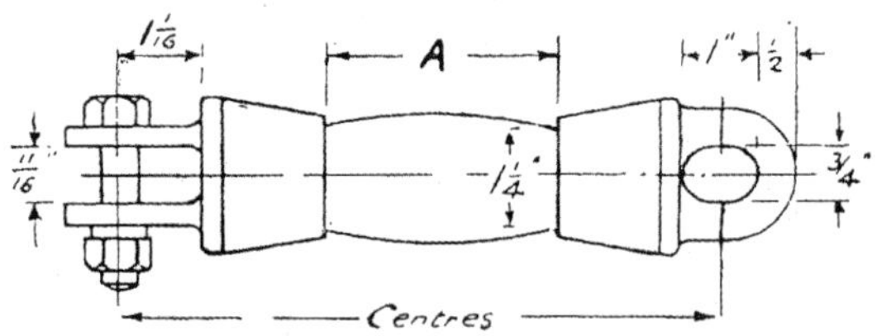

Eye and Clevis Type

A inch	Length of Wood	Centres inch	Weight lb.	Part No.
3	$5\frac{3}{4}$	$7\frac{13}{16}$	2.72	AA 90-262 Fig. 1
5	$7\frac{3}{4}$	$9\frac{13}{16}$	2.81	,, ,, ,, 2
7	$9\frac{3}{4}$	$11\frac{13}{16}$	2.90	,, ,, ,, 3
9	$11\frac{3}{4}$	$13\frac{13}{16}$	2.99	,, ,, ,, 4

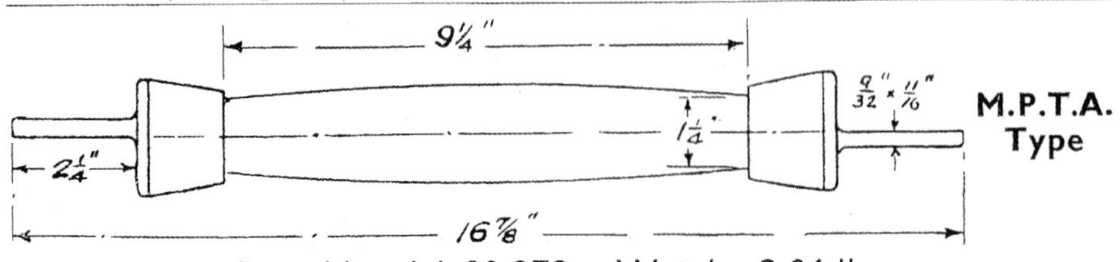

M.P.T.A. Type

Part No. AA 90-279. Weight 2.06 lb.

A15

Maps

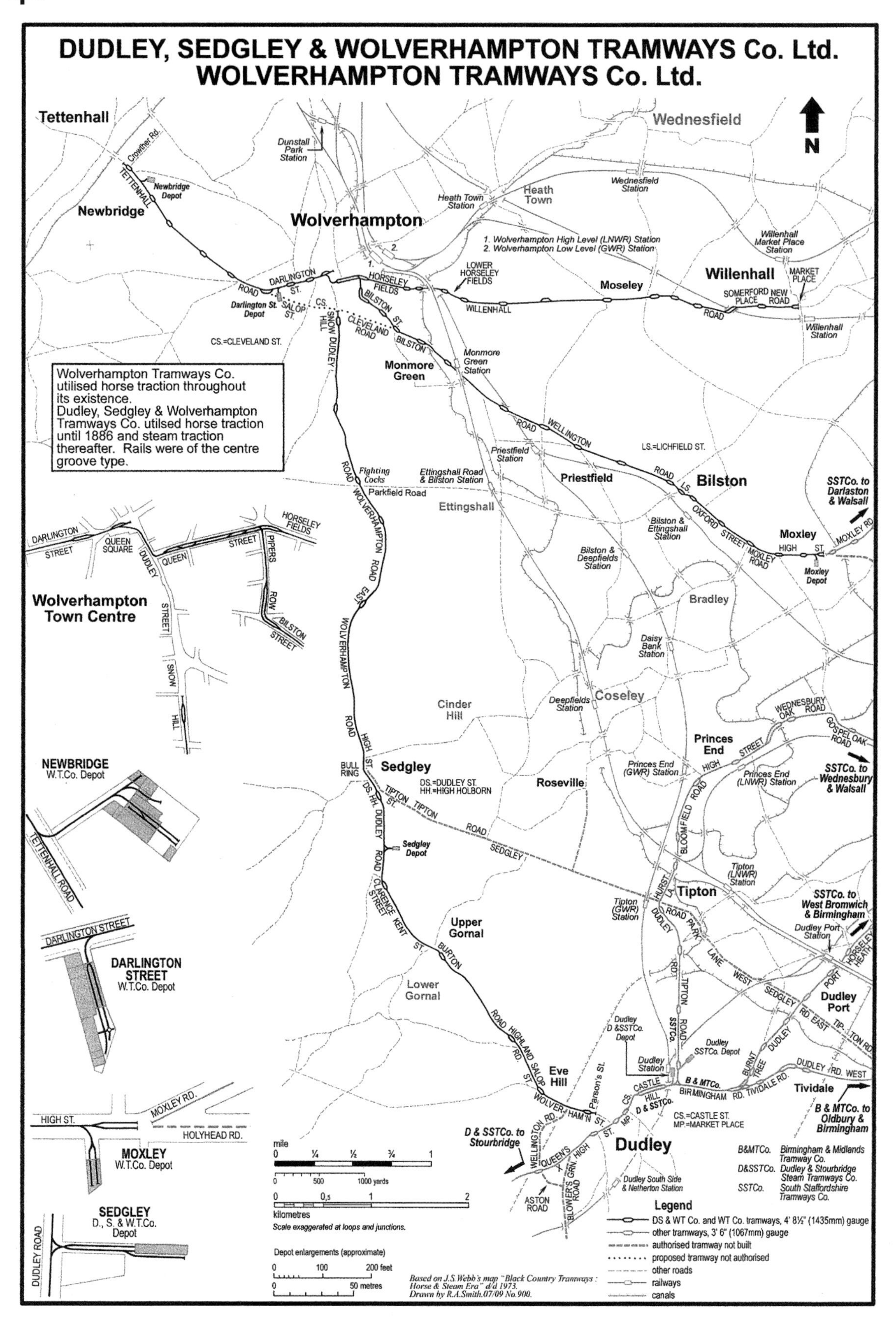
DUDLEY, SEDGLEY & WOLVERHAMPTON TRAMWAYS Co. Ltd.
WOLVERHAMPTON TRAMWAYS Co. Ltd.
N
Tettenhall
Newbridge
Newbridge Depot
Crowther Rd.
TETTENHALL
Dunstall Park Station
Wolverhampton
Heath Town Station
Heath Town
Wednesfield
Wednesfield Station
1. Wolverhampton High Level (LNWR) Station
2. Wolverhampton Low Level (GWR) Station
Willenhall Market Place Station
Willenhall
MARKET PLACE
SOMERFORD PLACE
NEW ROAD
Willenhall Station
Moseley
LOWER HORSELEY FIELDS
WILLENHALL
ROAD
DARLINGTON ST.
HORSELEY FIELDS
Darlington St. Depot
SALOP ST.
CS.
BILSTON ST.
CLEVELAND ROAD
SNOW HILL
DUDLEY
CS.=CLEVELAND ST.
Monmore Green
Monmore Green Station
Wolverhampton Tramways Co. utilised horse traction throughout its existence. Dudley, Sedgley & Wolverhampton Tramways Co. utilsed horse traction until 1886 and steam traction thereafter. Rails were of the centre groove type.
WELLINGTON ROAD
LS.=LICHFIELD ST.
Priestfield Station
Priestfield
Bilston
Fighting Cocks
Ettingshall Road & Bilston Station
Parkfield Road
Ettingshall
SSTCo. to Darlaston & Walsall
OXFORD STREET
Bilston & Ettingshall Station
Moxley
HIGH ST.
MOXLEY RD.
MOXLEY ROAD
Moxley Depot
Bilston & Deepfields Station
Bradley
Daisy Bank Station
WOLVERHAMPTON ROAD EAST
DARLINGTON STREET
QUEEN SQUARE
QUEEN STREET
PIPERS ROW
BILSTON STREET
DUDLEY STREET
SNOW HILL
Wolverhampton Town Centre
Cinder Hill
Deepfields Station
Coseley
WEDNESBURY OAK ROAD
GOSPEL OAK ROAD
Princes End
HIGH STREET
Princes End (GWR) Station
Princes End (LNWR) Station
SSTCo. to Wednesbury & Walsall
NEWBRIDGE
W.T.Co. Depot
TETTENHALL ROAD
BULL RING
HIGH ST.
Sedgley
DS.=DUDLEY ST.
HH.=HIGH HOLBORN
TIPTON ROAD
SEDGLEY
Roseville
Sedgley Depot
BLOOMFIELD ROAD
Tipton (LNWR) Station
Tipton
Tipton (GWR) Station
HURST LA.
DUDLEY ROAD
PARK LANE WEST
SSTCo. to West Bromwich & Birmingham
Dudley Port Station
HORSELEY HEATH
DARLINGTON STREET
DARLINGTON STREET
W.T.Co. Depot
CLARENCE STREET
KENT ST.
Upper Gornal
BURTON ROAD
Lower Gornal
SEDGLEY RD. EAST
Dudley Port
TIPTON ROAD
Dudley D.&SSTCo. Depot
Dudley SSTCo. Depot
BURNT TREE
DUDLEY RD. WEST
HIGHLAND ROAD
SALOP ST.
Eve Hill
Parson's St.
Dudley Station
B & MTCo.
BIRMINGHAM RD.
TIVIDALE RD.
Tividale
CASTLE HILL
D & SSTCo.
WOLVERHAMPTON ST.
B & MTCo. to Oldbury & Birmingham
CS.=CASTLE ST.
MP.=MARKET PLACE
HIGH ST.
HOLYHEAD RD.
MOXLEY
W.T.Co. Depot
mile
0 ¼ ½ ¾ 1
0 500 1000 yards
0 0.5 1 2
kilometres
Scale exaggerated at loops and junctions.
D & SSTCo. to Stourbridge
WELLINGTON RD.
QUEEN'S CROSS
ASTON ROAD
BLOWER'S GRN. ROAD
Dudley
Dudley South Side & Netherton Station
B&MTCo. Birmingham & Midlands Tramway Co.
D&SSTCo. Dudley & Stourbridge Steam Tramways Co.
SSTCo. South Staffordshire Tramways Co.
SEDGLEY
D., S. & W.T.Co. Depot
DUDLEY ROAD
Depot enlargements (approximate)
0 100 200 feet
0 50 metres
Based on J.S. Webb's map "Black Country Tramways : Horse & Steam Era" d'd 1973.
Drawn by R.A.Smith.07/09 No.900.
Legend
DS & WT Co. and WT Co. tramways, 4' 8½" (1435mm) gauge
other tramways, 3' 6" (1067mm) gauge
authorised tramway not built
proposed tramway not authorised
other roads
railways
canals

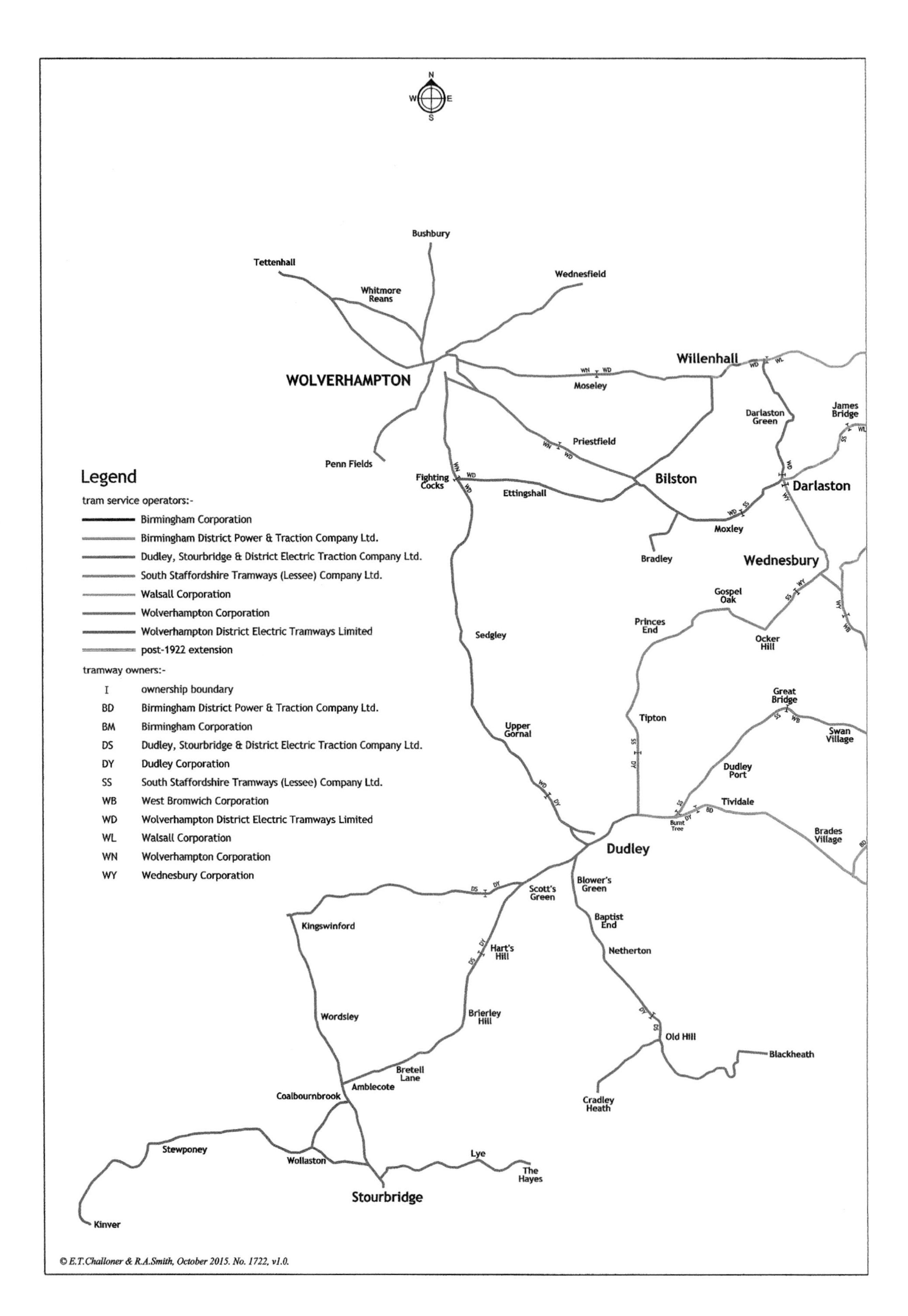
N
W
E
S
Bushbury
Tettenhall
Whitmore Reans
Wednesfield
WOLVERHAMPTON
Willenhall
Moseley
Penn Fields
Priestfield
Fighting Cocks
Ettingshall
Bilston
Darlaston Green
James Bridge
Darlaston
Moxley
Bradley
Wednesbury
Gospel Oak
Princes End
Ocker Hill
Sedgley
Tipton
Great Bridge
Swan Village
Upper Gornal
Dudley Port
Tividale
Burnt Tree
Brades Village
Dudley
Blower's Green
Scott's Green
Baptist End
Kingswinford
Hart's Hill
Netherton
Wordsley
Brierley Hill
Old Hill
Blackheath
Bretell Lane
Amblecote
Coalbournbrook
Cradley Heath
Stewponey
Wollaston
Lye
The Hayes
Stourbridge
Kinver
Legend
tram service operators:-
Birmingham Corporation
Birmingham District Power & Traction Company Ltd.
Dudley, Stourbridge & District Electric Traction Company Ltd.
South Staffordshire Tramways (Lessee) Company Ltd.
Walsall Corporation
Wolverhampton Corporation
Wolverhampton District Electric Tramways Limited
post-1922 extension
tramway owners:-
I ownership boundary
BD Birmingham District Power & Traction Company Ltd.
BM Birmingham Corporation
DS Dudley, Stourbridge & District Electric Traction Company Ltd.
DY Dudley Corporation
SS South Staffordshire Tramways (Lessee) Company Ltd.
WB West Bromwich Corporation
WD Wolverhampton District Electric Tramways Limited
WL Walsall Corporation
WN Wolverhampton Corporation
WY Wednesbury Corporation
© E.T.Challoner & R.A.Smith, October 2015. No. 1722, v1.0.

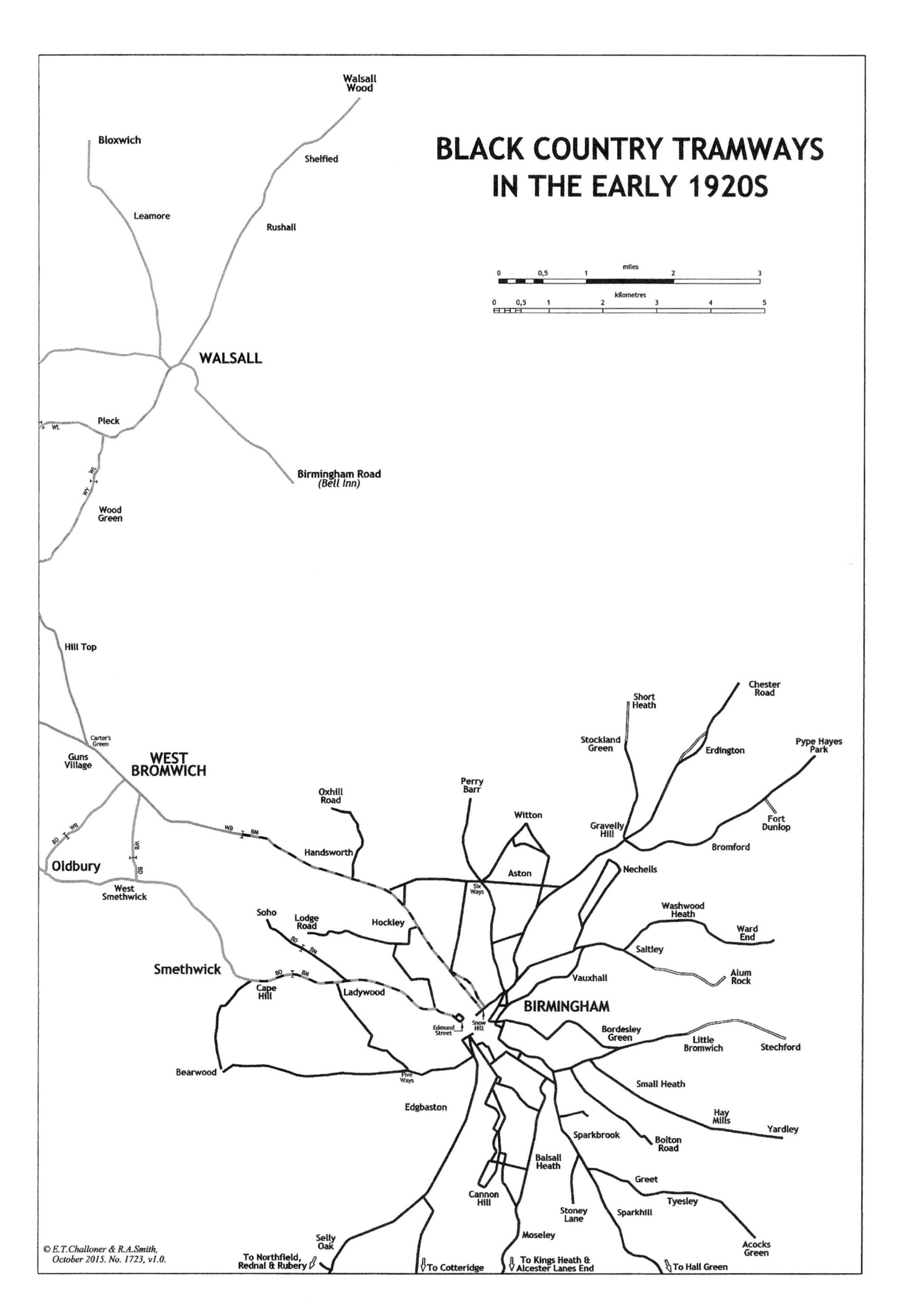
BLACK COUNTRY TRAMWAYS
IN THE EARLY 1920S
miles
0
0,5
1
2
3
kilometres
0
0,5
1
2
3
4
5
Walsall Wood
Bloxwich
Shelfied
Leamore
Rushall
WALSALL
Pleck
Birmingham Road
(Bell Inn)
Wood Green
Hill Top
Carter's Green
Guns Village
WEST BROMWICH
Oldbury
West Smethwick
Smethwick
Soho
Lodge Road
Hockley
Oxhill Road
Handsworth
Perry Barr
Witton
Aston
Six Ways
Short Heath
Stockland Green
Chester Road
Erdington
Pype Hayes Park
Gravelly Hill
Fort Dunlop
Bromford
Nechells
Washwood Heath
Ward End
Saltley
Alum Rock
Vauxhall
BIRMINGHAM
Cape Hill
Ladywood
Edmund Street
Snow Hill
Bearwood
Five Ways
Edgbaston
Bordesley Green
Little Bromwich
Stechford
Small Heath
Hay Mills
Yardley
Sparkbrook
Bolton Road
Balsall Heath
Greet
Tyesley
Cannon Hill
Stoney Lane
Sparkhill
Moseley
Acocks Green
Selly Oak
To Northfield, Rednal & Rubery
To Cotteridge
To Kings Heath & Alcester Lanes End
To Hall Green
© E.T.Challoner & R.A.Smith,
October 2015. No. 1723, v1.0.

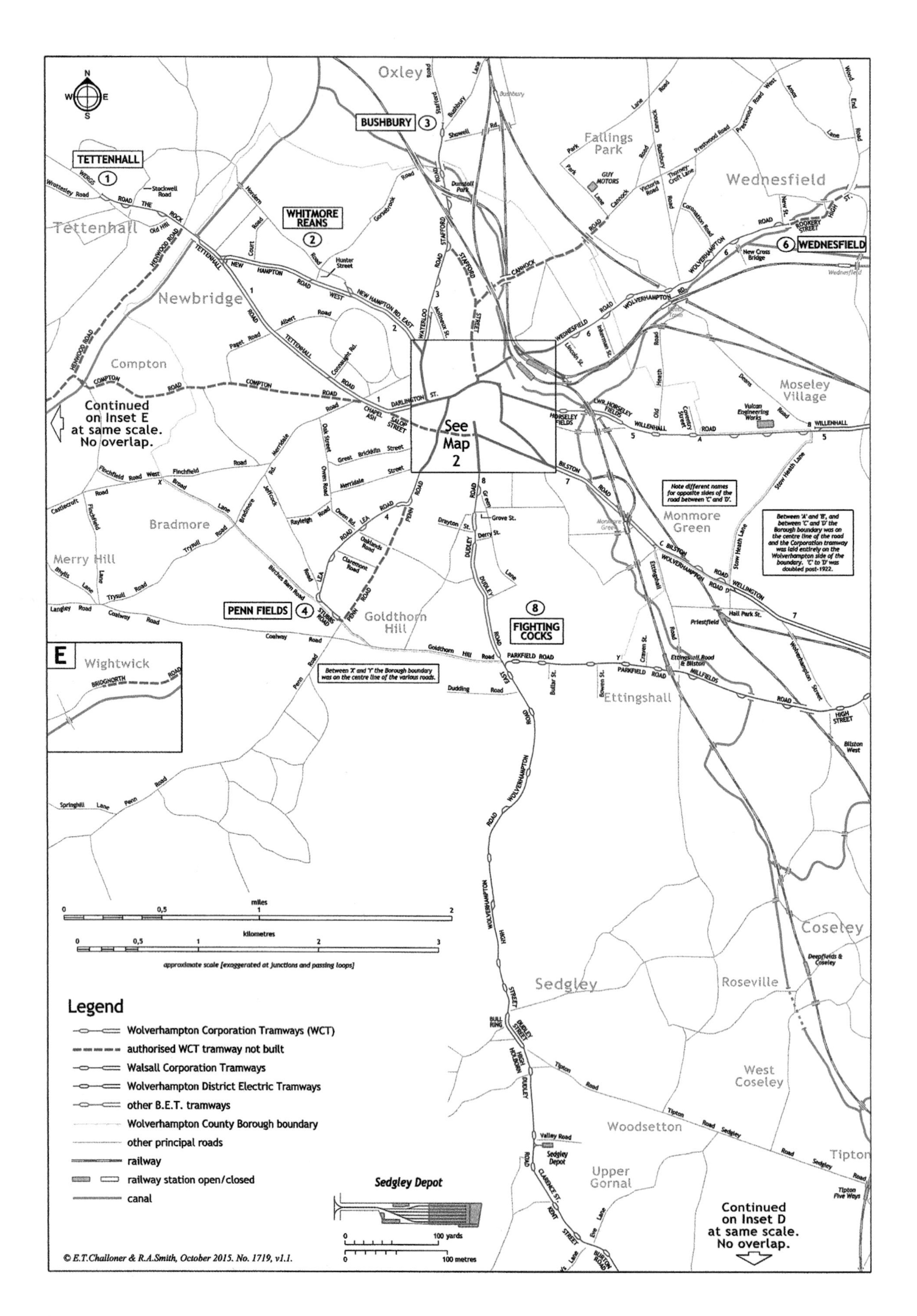
TETTENHALL 1
WHITMORE REANS 2
BUSHBURY 3
PENN FIELDS 4
WEDNESFIELD 6
FIGHTING COCKS 8
See Map 2
Continued on Inset E at same scale. No overlap.
Continued on Inset D at same scale. No overlap.
Oxley
Fallings Park
Wednesfield
Tettenhall
Newbridge
Compton
Moseley Village
Monmore Green
Bradmore
Merry Hill
Goldthorn Hill
Ettingshall
Wightwick
Coseley
Sedgley
Roseville
West Coseley
Woodsetton
Upper Gornal
Tipton
GUY MOTORS
Vulcan Engineering Works
Note different names for opposite sides of the road between 'C' and 'D'.
Between 'A' and 'B', and between 'C' and 'D' the Borough boundary was on the centre line of the road and the Corporation tramway was laid entirely on the Wolverhampton side of the boundary. 'C' to 'D' was doubled post-1922.
Between 'X' and 'Y' the Borough boundary was on the centre line of the various roads.
Sedgley Depot
miles
kilometres
approximate scale [exaggerated at junctions and passing loops]
Legend
Wolverhampton Corporation Tramways (WCT)
authorised WCT tramway not built
Walsall Corporation Tramways
Wolverhampton District Electric Tramways
other B.E.T. tramways
Wolverhampton County Borough boundary
other principal roads
railway
railway station open/closed
canal
© E.T.Challoner & R.A.Smith, October 2015. No. 1719, v1.1.

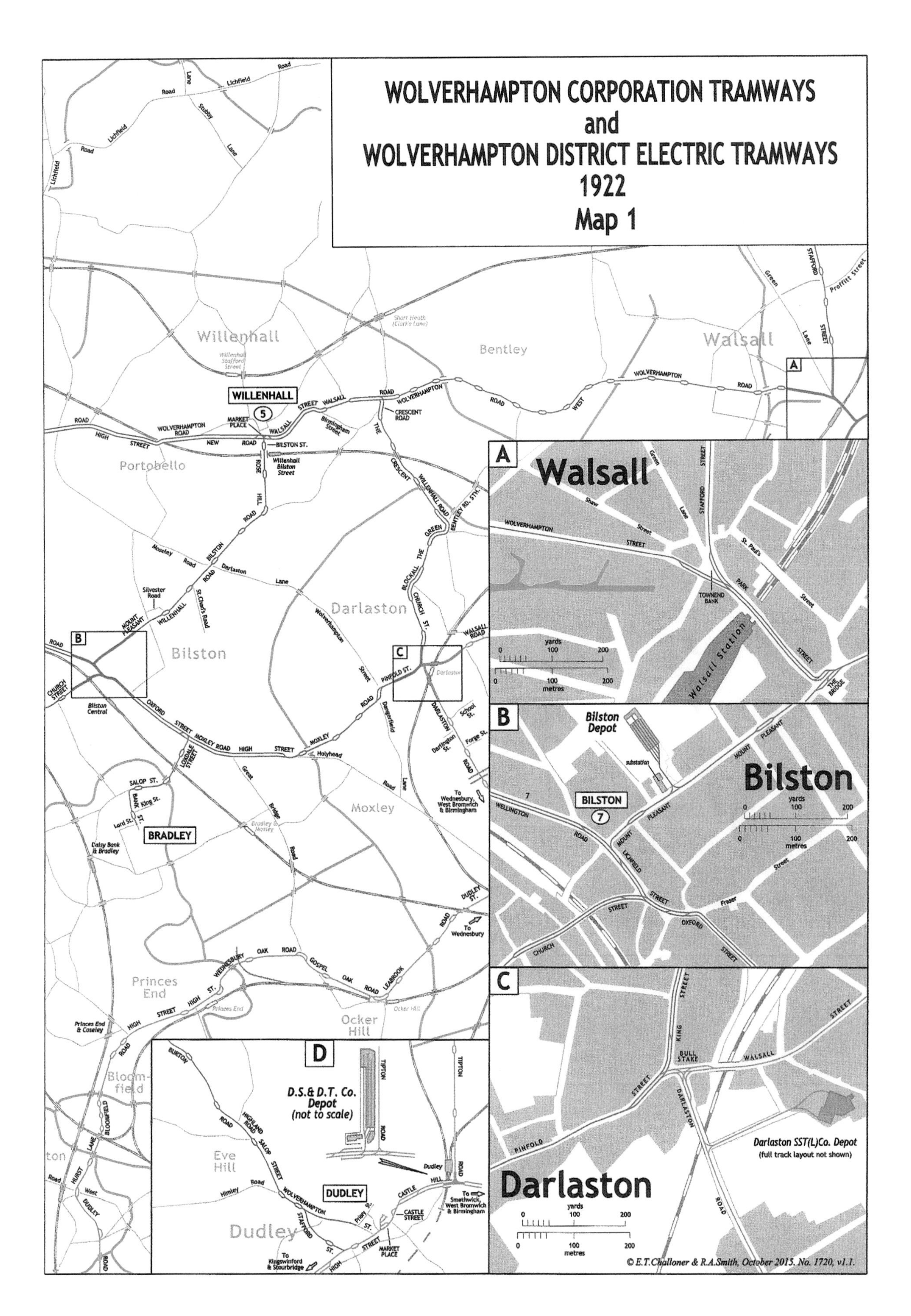
WOLVERHAMPTON CORPORATION TRAMWAYS
and
WOLVERHAMPTON DISTRICT ELECTRIC TRAMWAYS
1922
Map 1
Willenhall
Bentley
Walsall
WILLENHALL
Portobello
Darlaston
Bilston
Moxley
BRADLEY
Princes End
Ocker Hill
Bloomfield
Eve Hill
Dudley
DUDLEY
D.S.& D.T. Co. Depot (not to scale)
A
Walsall
Walsall Station
B
Bilston Depot
Bilston
BILSTON
C
Darlaston
Darlaston SST(L)Co. Depot (full track layout not shown)
D
© E.T.Challoner & R.A.Smith, October 2015. No. 1720, v1.1.

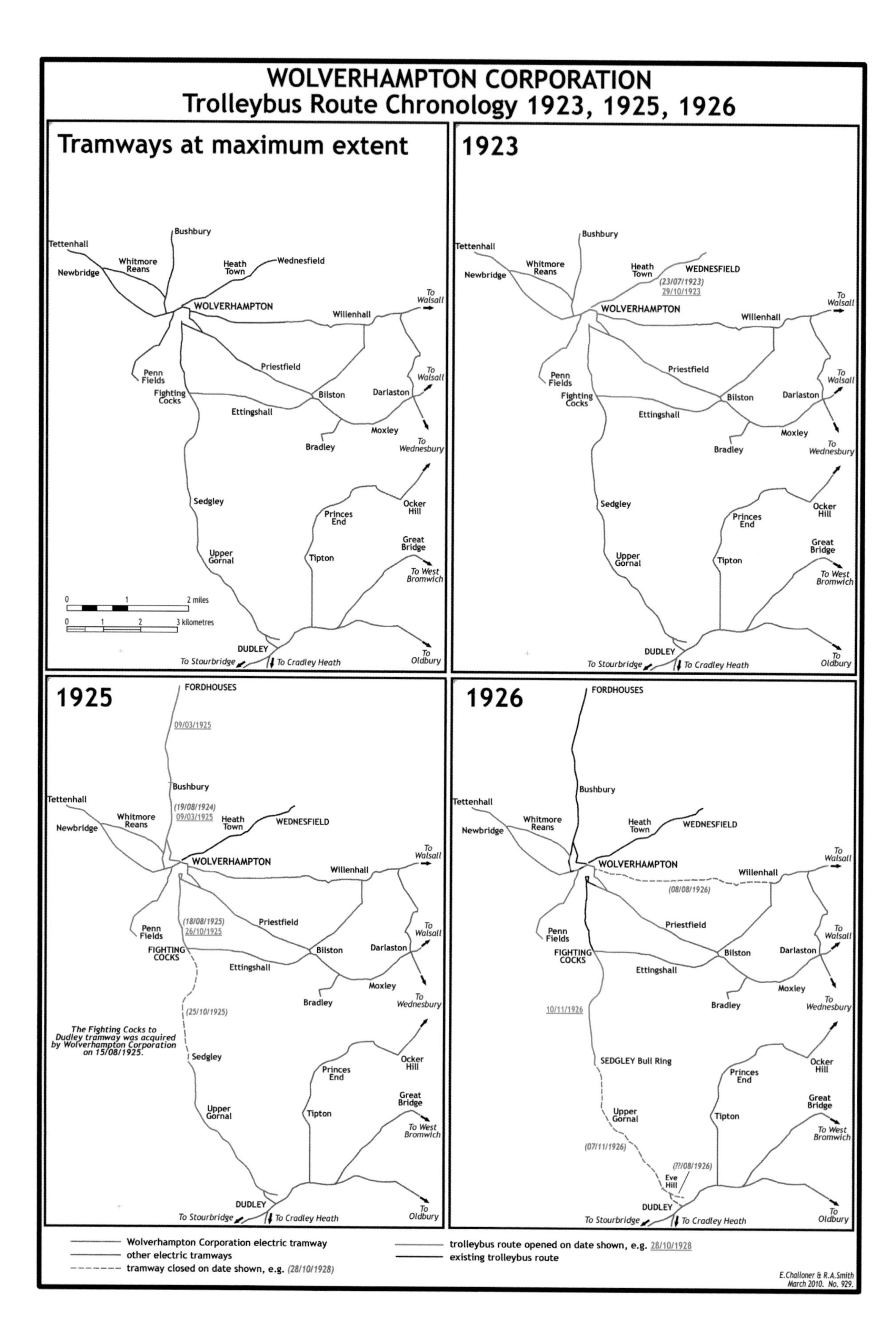
WOLVERHAMPTON CORPORATION
Trolleybus Route Chronology 1923, 1925, 1926
Tramways at maximum extent
1923
1925
1926
Tettenhall
Newbridge
Whitmore Reans
Bushbury
Heath Town
Wednesfield
WEDNESFIELD
WOLVERHAMPTON
Willenhall
To Walsall
Priestfield
Penn Fields
Fighting Cocks
FIGHTING COCKS
Bilston
Darlaston
Ettingshall
Moxley
Bradley
To Wednesbury
Sedgley
SEDGLEY Bull Ring
Ocker Hill
Princes End
Great Bridge
Upper Gornal
Tipton
To West Bromwich
Eve Hill
DUDLEY
To Stourbridge
To Cradley Heath
To Oldbury
FORDHOUSES
(23/07/1923)
29/10/1923
09/03/1925
(19/08/1924)
09/03/1925
(18/08/1925)
26/10/1925
(25/10/1925)
The Fighting Cocks to Dudley tramway was acquired by Wolverhampton Corporation on 15/08/1925.
(08/08/1926)
10/11/1926
(07/11/1926)
(??/08/1926)
0 1 2 miles
0 1 2 3 kilometres
Wolverhampton Corporation electric tramway
other electric tramways
tramway closed on date shown, e.g. (28/10/1928)
trolleybus route opened on date shown, e.g. 28/10/1928
existing trolleybus route
E.Challoner & R.A.Smith
March 2010. No. 929.

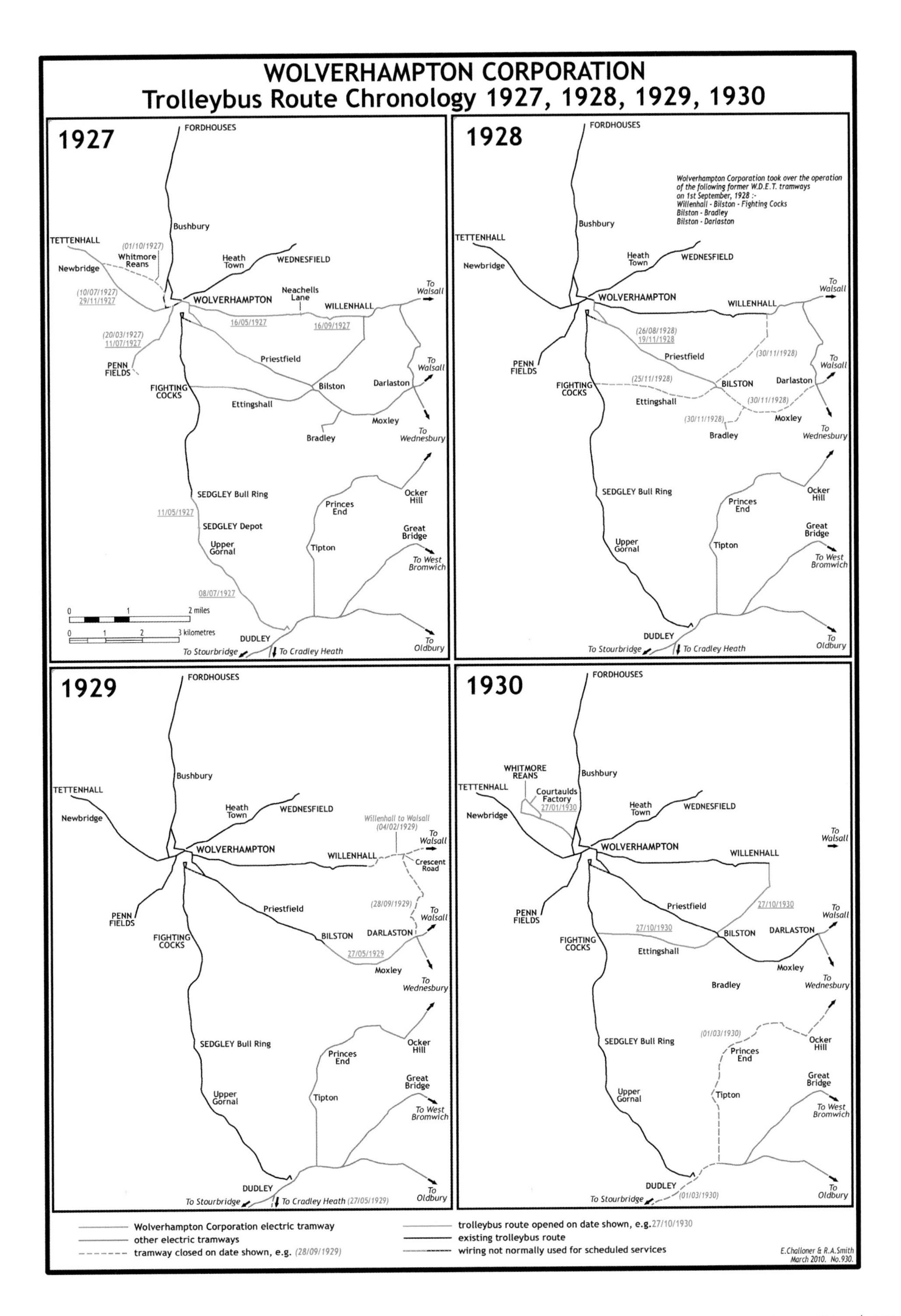

WOLVERHAMPTON CORPORATION
Trolleybus Route Chronology 1927, 1928, 1929, 1930
1927
FORDHOUSES
Bushbury
TETTENHALL
(01/10/1927)
Whitmore Reans
Newbridge
Heath Town
WEDNESFIELD
(10/07/1927)
29/11/1927
WOLVERHAMPTON
Neachells Lane
To Walsall
WILLENHALL
16/05/1927
16/09/1927
(20/03/1927)
11/07/1927
Priestfield
PENN FIELDS
To Walsall
FIGHTING COCKS
Bilston
Darlaston
Ettingshall
Moxley
Bradley
To Wednesbury
SEDGLEY Bull Ring
Princes End
Ocker Hill
11/05/1927
SEDGLEY Depot
Great Bridge
Upper Gornal
Tipton
To West Bromwich
08/07/1927
0 1 2 miles
0 1 2 3 kilometres
DUDLEY
To Stourbridge
To Cradley Heath
To Oldbury
1928
FORDHOUSES
Wolverhampton Corporation took over the operation of the following former W.D.E.T. tramways on 1st September, 1928 :-
Willenhall - Bilston - Fighting Cocks
Bilston - Bradley
Bilston - Darlaston
Bushbury
TETTENHALL
Newbridge
Heath Town
WEDNESFIELD
To Walsall
WOLVERHAMPTON
WILLENHALL
(26/08/1928)
19/11/1928
Priestfield
(30/11/1928)
PENN FIELDS
To Walsall
FIGHTING COCKS
(25/11/1928)
BILSTON
Darlaston
Ettingshall
(30/11/1928)
(30/11/1928)
Moxley
Bradley
To Wednesbury
SEDGLEY Bull Ring
Ocker Hill
Princes End
Great Bridge
Upper Gornal
Tipton
To West Bromwich
DUDLEY
To Stourbridge
To Cradley Heath
To Oldbury
1929
FORDHOUSES
Bushbury
TETTENHALL
Newbridge
Heath Town
WEDNESFIELD
Willenhall to Walsall
(04/02/1929)
To Walsall
WOLVERHAMPTON
WILLENHALL
Crescent Road
(28/09/1929)
Priestfield
To Walsall
PENN FIELDS
BILSTON
DARLASTON
FIGHTING COCKS
27/05/1929
Moxley
To Wednesbury
SEDGLEY Bull Ring
Ocker Hill
Princes End
Great Bridge
Upper Gornal
Tipton
To West Bromwich
DUDLEY
To Stourbridge
To Cradley Heath (27/05/1929)
To Oldbury
1930
FORDHOUSES
WHITMORE REANS
Bushbury
TETTENHALL
Courtaulds Factory
27/01/1930
Heath Town
WEDNESFIELD
Newbridge
To Walsall
WOLVERHAMPTON
WILLENHALL
Priestfield
27/10/1930
To Walsall
PENN FIELDS
27/10/1930
BILSTON
DARLASTON
FIGHTING COCKS
Ettingshall
Moxley
Bradley
To Wednesbury
(01/03/1930)
SEDGLEY Bull Ring
Ocker Hill
Princes End
Great Bridge
Upper Gornal
Tipton
To West Bromwich
DUDLEY
To Stourbridge
(01/03/1930)
To Oldbury
Wolverhampton Corporation electric tramway
other electric tramways
tramway closed on date shown, e.g. (28/09/1929)
trolleybus route opened on date shown, e.g. 27/10/1930
existing trolleybus route
wiring not normally used for scheduled services
E.Challoner & R.A.Smith
March 2010. No.930.

WOLVERHAMPTON CORPORATION TRAMWAYS

Central Area - 1922

Map 2

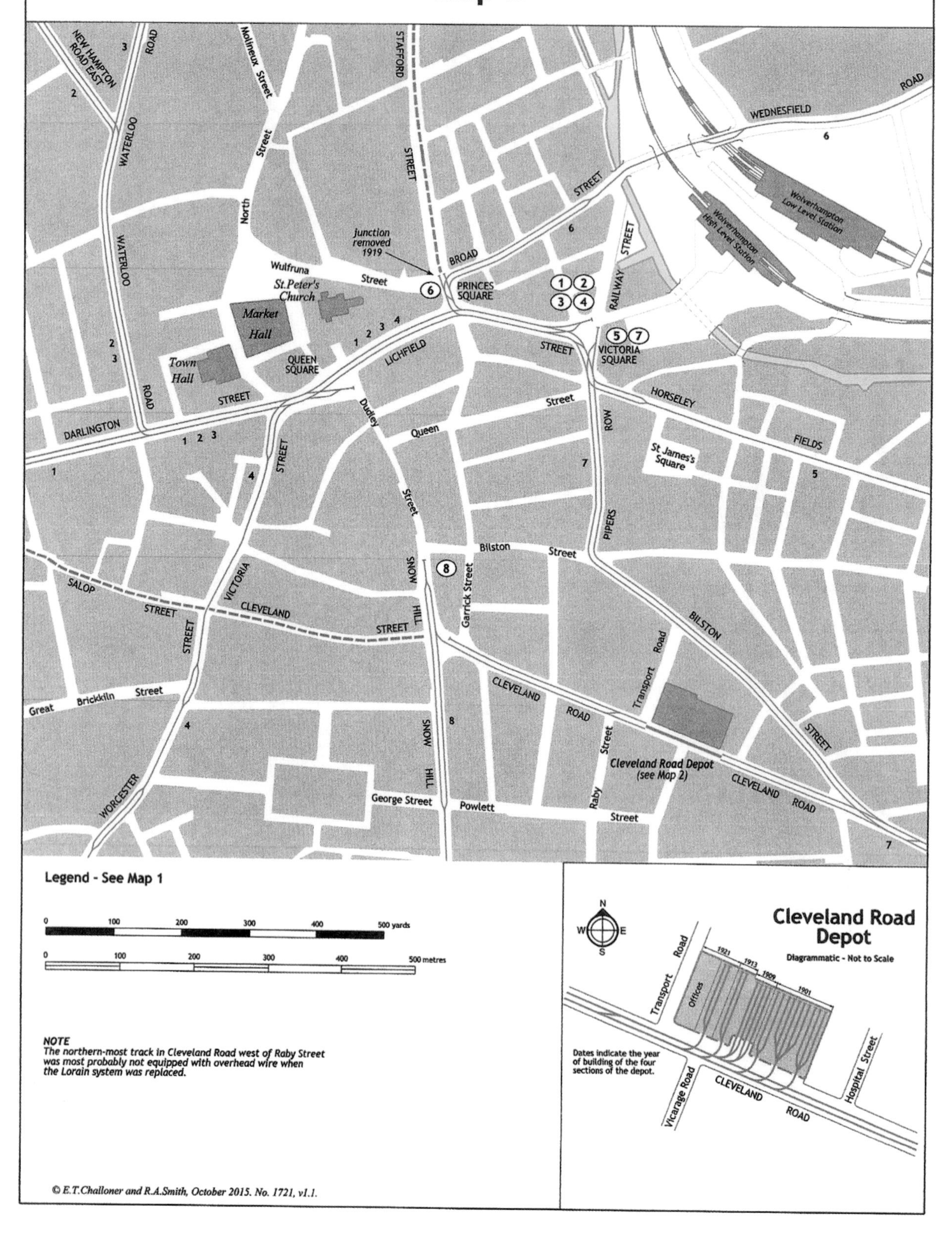